LITERARY LUMINARIES *of* *the* BERKSHIRES

LITERARY LUMINARIES *of* *the* BERKSHIRES

FROM HERMAN MELVILLE TO PATRICIA HIGHSMITH

BERNARD A. DREW

Foreword by Ronald Latham, Director, Berkshire Athenaeum

THE
History
PRESS

Published by The History Press
Charleston, SC 29403
www.historypress.net

Bottom middle front cover image: W.E.B. Du Bois. *Courtesy of the Library of Congress.*
Middle back cover image: Henry David Thoreau spent a night atop Mount Greylock in 1844.
It's the highest point in Massachusetts. *Bernard A. Drew.*

First published 2015

Manufactured in the United States

ISBN 978.1.62619.877.7

Library of Congress Control Number: 2015937273

Notice: The information in this book is true and complete to the best of our knowledge. It is
offered without guarantee on the part of the author or The History Press. The author and
The History Press disclaim all liability in connection with the use of this book.

CONTENTS

CONTENTS

FOREWORD

I've been a public library director for thirty-six years, with three libraries under my belt before I traveled to Pittsfield twenty-two years ago, so I can attest from personal experience that public libraries collect the works of local authors as part of a local history mission. The Berkshire Athenaeum's strategic planning consistently ranks local history service as one of our top five roles, a service that targets the desire of visitors to know and better understand personal or community heritage. One of four goals in our action plan stipulates, "People from around the world will be provided the resources to explore personal, historical and cultural heritage, including the works of notable Berkshire authors." The creative output of Berkshire authors is such an integral part of our history and heritage, from titans like Melville and Hawthorne to the more obscure, like Harlan Ballard, one of my predecessors as director of the Berkshire Athenaeum. People who study the history of the Berkshires cannot help but stumble over the authors who flocked to the scenic Berkshire region in western Massachusetts once dubbed the "American Lake District" because of the prevalence of the literary and artistic elite.

It is because the Berkshires attracted and inspired such a rich assortment of writers for well over two hundred years that the Berkshire Athenaeum amassed a collection of more than four thousand items by local authors. While that may appear to be a lot for the Berkshires to be proud of, Bernard A. Drew's research makes us painfully aware that our collection only scratches the surface of the Berkshires' literary talent. While the librarians in the Local History Department of the Athenaeum know a lot about Berkshire authors, they have benefited tremendously for almost thirty years from Bernie's scholarship on the topic. His very considerable personal contribution to local history bibliography aside, he is, after all, a regular newspaper columnist and the author of Berkshire histories, including books about Great Barrington, Monument Mountain, Lake Buel, Beartown, the Knox Trail and the Housatonic River. In 1985, he compiled *Berkshire Between Covers: A Literary History*, an annotated catalogue of some 210 fiction writers and poets from the Berkshires that became a touch point for library staff digging for information about Berkshire writers. Eleven years later, *Berkshire Between Covers: Page Two* was released (of which only a few dozen copies were distributed) and grew that catalogue to 850 prose writers, dramatists, poets and lyricists, and for the past eighteen years this then became the foundation for Athenaeum librarians answering reference inquiries pertaining to writers in the Berkshires.

With *Literary Luminaries of the Berkshires: From Herman Melville to Patricia Highsmith*, Bernie has again revisited the topic, but with rather dramatic changes. With an estimated 250 writers included, he is selective in his coverage, focusing again exclusively on writers of fiction and poetry but this time choosing to arrange his material thematically, giving him the opportunity to digress beautifully into more extensive background notes, contextual anecdotes and humorous jibes that allow him to play to his strengths as the foremost historian of the Berkshires. So read on, and enjoy how Bernie provides a unique perspective on local history by bringing Berkshire authors to life.

—RONALD LATHAM, DIRECTOR
Berkshire Athenaeum, Pittsfield's Public Library

INTRODUCTION

L et's assemble a library, a special library of fiction writers, dramatists and poets who are linked to Berkshire County in western Massachusetts. Whether natives, transplants, visitors or complete strangers, most of these writers have incorporated the area's natural setting into their stories or verses.

We include early American writers, landmark writers, everyday toiling writers and leisurely writers. A few will receive particular scrutiny. We'll hear about William Cullen Bryant's health regimen. We'll search for Herman Melville's piazza. We'll roam Charles Pierce Burton's Adams as depicted in his boys' adventure books. We'll share travails with Mark Twain in Tyringham. We'll climb mountains with Henry David Thoreau, loll by the Housatonic River with Henry Wadsworth Longfellow and buzz around the county's roads with Edith Wharton. We'll sing a joyous carol with Edmund Hamilton Sears.

Genre writers have come to the fore: mystery, science fiction, romance, western and juvenile authors such as Amanda Cross, Nancy Thayer, Archer Mayor, Rachel Field and Bill Gulick have places in our library along with poets such as Louise Gluck, Joyce Kilmer and James Taylor.

We will learn about writers' deeper connections with the Berkshires.

Few of these wordsmiths were born here. The Berkshire hills, rather, are a cultural magnet. The area appeals to writers, poets and artists who mostly work in isolation. They don't need to know each other; they just need to know the landscape nurtures their creative soul. There's no single Berkshire style or message. But there is a Berkshire spirit and vibrancy.

There is a continuum. Writers beginning with the Fireside Poets and carrying on with the Young Americans through the modern day have established a distinct literature. They have not only kept up with trends, they have established them.

Over the years, I've accumulated a file drawer full of newspaper cuttings and notes about Berkshire literature. I've prowled public and university libraries and new and secondhand bookstores. I've examined hundreds of books. As a weekly newspaper reporter, editor and columnist and as a reference book author and local historian, I've spoken to or exchanged e-mails with many writers. So I've appointed myself librarian.

It's time to stock our shelves.

—Bernard A. Drew

I
LITERARY PIONEERS

In far western Massachusetts in the late eighteenth century, two women and two men were the first to express themselves in verse and prose. Two names have endured; two are unfamiliar.

FIRST NEWSPAPER POET: "PHILO SAPPHO"

Seven poems appeared in Hartford's *Connecticut Courant* in the years 1771–74 written by "Philo Sappho"—a merging of the names of an ancient Jewish philosopher and a female Greek lyric poet. These verses are the earliest identified secular writings by a Berkshire resident. Historian Lion G. Miles, who found the verses rather morbid and sad, makes a good circumstantial case that Anna Dix Bingham (1745–1817) was the author. One poem is about an event: "The following lines were occasioned by [the] sawing down of a Liberty tree in Great Barrington, on the night next after the 28th day of June last" (published July 26, 1774). A Watertown, Massachusetts native, Bingham was living in Great Barrington when the verses were published. Anna and her husband, Silas, moved to Stockbridge, where in 1778 they opened a tavern, predecessor to the Red Lion Inn on Main Street.

Most eighteenth-century newspaper verse was published anonymously or under pseudonym, and Bingham followed form. Berkshire County's earliest newspaper, the *Berkshire Chronicle*, issued in Pittsfield from 1788 to 1790, regularly carried verse by "Crispin" or "Philo Independence" or "Justus" or "Whipper." Who were they? "None of it was terribly good," scholar Ann Brunjes said. "Even the more polished pieces were pale imitations of British neo-classical verse, and the unpolished were nearly incomprehensible with allusions to local characters and events so obscure that only the most dogged contemporary reader could unearth their meanings."

FIRST BOOK POET: DAVID HITCHCOCK

Etheridge & Bliss of Boston issued *The Shade of Plato* in 1806, marking David Hitchcock Jr. (1773–1849) Berkshire's first book-published poet. "The Cobbler Poet," as he was known, was born in Bethlehem, Connecticut, and came to West Stockbridge in 1793 to work as a shoemaker. He relocated to Great Barrington, where, according to the book's preface, "He began the practice of scribbling, which was his favorite amusement, very early. Some of his first productions were paraphrases on the thirty-ninth Psalm."

Appleton's Encyclopedia said the book "is written with ease and smoothness, and closes with expostulations on the revolutionary principles in vogue at the beginning of the century."

Scholar Richard Birdsall sighed, "Unfortunately, Hitchcock could never feel at home in abstract thought, and as a result, his diction rarely manages to be anything but stilted and unimaginative."

Little is known of Hitchcock's later life. He published three more books, including *A Political Dictionary* (1808). He died in Iowa.

FIRST PUBLISHED SHORT STORY WRITER: WILLIAM CULLEN BRYANT

William Cullen Bryant (1794–1878) was one of America's early Fireside Poets whose works were frequently memorized by schoolchildren.

Bryant was born in Cummington. "As a youth, Cullen was frail and sometimes sickly; indeed, when he was a baby his father had despaired of rearing him and subjected him to the heroic treatment of immersion in cold water to toughen him," Gerard Chapman said.

Dad dunked Cully head-down in the horse trough.

Bryant began to write poems when he was eight. His anti-Jefferson *The Embargo, or, Sketches of the Times, a Satire by a Youth of Thirteen*, with his father's encouragement, was published as a twelve-page pamphlet. Bryant attended Williams College. He began "Thanatopsis" when he was seventeen; a visit to the rippling stream at Flora's Glen off Bee Hill Road likely inspired its completion during his sophomore year at Williams. It was a milestone in American literature, though poet laureate Richard Wilbur doesn't think the poem holds up: "'Thanatopsis,' which my father took pleasure in declaiming over the shaving bowl, is another poem in which elevation of style masks from the reader and from the poet the insufficiency of its argument."

Admitted to the bar when he was nineteen, Bryant struggled to practice law in Great Barrington from 1816 to 1825. He was town clerk, justice of the peace, hog reeve, school committeeman and tithingman for the Congregational church.

Bryant's first book, *Poems* (1821), brought him notice but little income—$14.92, to be exact. He did find a life mate, Frances Fairchild of Alford, who had "the sweetest smile I had ever seen." They exchanged vows in the front room of the Dwight-Henderson House in 1821 and then took quarters from the Widow Ives on Taylor Hill. Rent was $30.00 a year plus $0.17 a week to pasture a cow.

His years in Great Barrington were fruitful—the environs inspired "Green River" (1819), "Monument Mountain" (1824) and "An Indian at the Burial Place of His Fathers" (1824). He based "The Murdered Traveller" on a real incident from the winter of 1808.

But he was disappointed in the lack of cultural energy. Through his friend Charles Sedgwick, Bryant got to know the latter's sister, Catharine, and her circle. He was lured to New York City in 1826 to become editor of the *New York Review*. He wrote short stories for the *United States Review and Literary Gazette*, including "A Border Tradition" (1826), the earliest short story by a Berkshire resident and with a Berkshire setting—Great Barrington. The Irving-esque story is about English settler James Williams's slack-paced courtship of a Dutch woman, Mary Suydam, and of the unusual way her sister Geshie uses superstition to bring the romance to fruition.

Bryant became outspoken editor of the *New York Post*, decrying bank monopolies, supporting labor unions and advocating for a Central Park. Henry Wadsworth Longfellow visited Bryant in New York in 1850 and chuckled in his journal, "Found him just beginning an article for his paper, in a kind of garret, surrounded by piles of newspapers and cheap novels. What a life!"

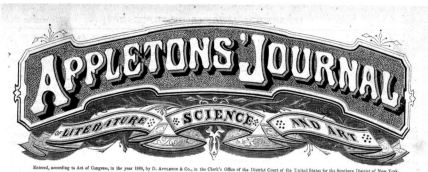

Entered, according to Act of Congress, in the year 1869, by D. APPLETON & Co., in the Clerk's Office of the District Court of the United States for the Southern District of New York.

No. 38.—VOL. II.]   SATURDAY, DECEMBER 18, 1869.   { PRICE TEN CENTS. { WITH STEEL ENGRAVING.

THE POET OF OUR WOODS.   BY W. J. HENNESSEY.

William Cullen Bryant's Great Barrington short story was set in a swamp across the road from the Dwight House, where he and his bride were married in 1821. Appletons' Journal, *1869.*

The Bryant Homestead in Cummington is a National Historic Landmark maintained by the Trustees of Reservations. Remington Hill in Cummington is sometimes called Mount Bryant. The Dwight-Henderson House and Taylor Hill in Great Barrington are privately owned today. Installation of a United States Geological Survey signal station on East Mountain in this town in 1884 prompted the suggestion (never made official) that it be renamed Mount Bryant.

Bryant's Wooden Dumbbells

In response to an inquiry from the editor of Herald of Health *in 1871, William Cullen Bryant described his exercise regimen and diet to invigorate mind and body.*

I rise early—at this time of year about half past five; in summer half an hour, or even an hour, earlier. Immediately, with very little encumbrance of clothing, I begin a series of exercises, for the most part designed to expand the chest, and at the same time to call into action all the muscles and articulations of the body. These are performed with dumb-bells—the very lightest, covered with flannel—with a pole, a horizontal bar, and a light chair swung around my head. After a full hour, and sometimes more, passed in this manner, I bathe from head to foot. When at my place in the country, I sometimes shorten my exercises in the chamber, and going out, occupy myself for half an hour or more in some work, which requires brisk exercise…

My breakfast is a simple one—hominy and milk, or in place of hominy, brown bread, or oat meal, or wheaten grits, and, in the season, baked sweet apples. Buckwheat cakes I do not decline, or any other article of vegetable food, but animal food I never take at breakfast. Tea and coffee I never touch at any time. Sometime I take a cup of chocolate, which has no narcotic effect, and agrees with me very well. At breakfast I often eat fruit, either in its natural state or freshly stewed…

In the country I dine early, and it is only at that meal that I take either meat or fish, and of these but a moderate quantity, making my dinner mostly of vegetables…My drink is water, yet I sometimes, though rarely, take a glass of wine. I am a natural temperance man, finding myself rather confused than exhilarated by wine. I never meddle with tobacco, except to quarrel with its use.

That I may rise early, I of course go to bed early; in town, as early as 10; in the country, sometimes earlier.

FIRST PUBLISHED NOVELIST: CATHARINE SEDGWICK

Catharine Maria Sedgwick (1789–1867) sparked a literary community.

"Miss Sedgwick was a highly intelligent woman…cultivated, bountiful and good, and her household was the center of the Berkshires. The naturalness of her style was a kind of triumph, and she prepared the way for the writers who followed by stimulating the interest of her readers in their own landscape and manners," Van Wyck Brooks wrote.

The daughter of Theodore and Pamela Dwight Sedgwick, Catharine was born in Stockbridge and educated at Boston and Albany boarding schools. A black woman named Mumbet, who was represented by Theodore in the 1781 court suit that earned her freedom from slavery, nannied Catharine and her brother Charles when their mother fell into severe depression. Catharine left the Berkshires after her mother's death and her father's second marriage. She mingled in New York's literary and social circles. After her father died in 1813, she returned to Stockbridge newly converted to Unitarianism. Her first novel, *A New England Tale* (1822), was spun from Stockbridge people and places. This and other works included moral instruction and protested religious intolerance.

"*A New England Tale* was recognized as one of the first novels to include authentic American settings, situations and characters," according to *American Women Writers from Colonial Times to the Present*. "It was soon a bestseller on both sides of the Atlantic. With the publication of *Redwood* (1824), Miss Sedgwick became as popular as her contemporaries Cooper and Irving…With her third novel, *Hope Leslie* (1827), Miss Sedgwick became the most famous American woman writer of her day."

"By its literary merit alone, *A New England Tale* raised Miss

Catharine Sedgwick worked Berkshire people and settings into her novels. *Library of Congress, Prints & Photographs Division.*

Sedgwick at once to the level and into the society of the leaders of a new and independent American literature," Chard Powers Smith said.

Sedgwick never married. She circulated between Stockbridge (her father's mansion), Lenox (brother Charles's home) and New York (brother Robert's home).

Sedgwick at first wasn't literarily keen on her hometown. She wrote in 1804: "Stockbridge is barren of incidents to call forth either wonder, admiration, or disgust. I sincerely believe there has nothing happened since your departure that has affected us as much, or appeared of half the importance, as some wounds which old Bose [the cow] has received."

But as she matured as a writer, Sedgwick made great use of Berkshire settings. *The Linwoods* (1835) examines the patriotic Lees of Massachusetts and aristocratic Linwoods of New York at the time of the American Revolution. She used local color before the term was coined.

There were few major American authors when Sedgwick's first book appeared anonymously, and one French publisher recklessly inserted James Fenimore Cooper's byline—despite his rugged outdoor adventures and her didactic prose having little in common.

Nathaniel Hawthorne, Washington Irving and Ralph Waldo Emerson sipped tea with her, as did European writers Harriet Martineau, Anna Jameson and Frederika Bremer.

"The Sedgwicks pervaded the Berkshires," Brooks remarked. "Everything happened at Lenox, and everyone came there."

The author's grave is in the Sedgwick Pie in Stockbridge Cemetery. The Sedgwick home on Main Street is still owned by the family.

SEDGWICK IN THE COAL BUSH

Catharine M. Sedgwick was curious about rural Berkshire ways. Her young adult book The Boy of Mount Rhigi (1848), as an example, is set against the backdrop of the iron industry and charcoaling and tells of young Clapham "Clap" Dunn, who picked up his thieving father's dirty habits. Can his friend Harry Davis save the boy from a grim future?

Near the summit of the mountain there is a furnace, and around it a scrambling village inhabited by colliers, and forgers, and the loafers [low fellows, she explained in a note] *who are usually attracted about a*

19

place of this description. Behind the village, and sunken rather below its level, and separated from it by an intervening morass, is a bit of water, precious to the sportsman, for it is excellent fishing-ground for sunfish, perch, and pickerel.

A reviewer wrote in the *Knickerbocker*:

This is a very charming, truthful little volume which we hope to see widely disseminated. It is the first of a series designed for the young people of our country…The volume is written to awaken in those of our young people who have been carefully nurtured a sense of their duty to those who are less favored; to show them that the ignorant, neglected, and apparently vicious have the germs of goodness in their souls; that patience, kindness and affection will fall like holy dew upon them, nourishing that which God has implanted.

The shorn forests have regrown since charcoaling days. The old Mount Riga furnace survives in Salisbury, Connecticut, an industrial monument. And the Sedgwick story has endured in an unexpected way—as a Christian radio drama from Lamplighter Theatre in 2010.

II

THE AMERICAN LAKE DISTRICT

Early Authors

Henry Ward Beecher is credited with calling the Berkshires the "American Lake District" for its abundance of littérateurs and artists. Beecher in *Star Papers* (1855) actually said, "From Salisbury to Williamstown, and then to Bennington in Vermont, there stretches a county of valleys, lakes and mountains, that is yet to be as celebrated as the lake-district of England and the hill-country of Palestine."

Western Massachusetts's many writers and poets drew obvious comparison to the Lake District of England associated with the Romantic poets William Wordsworth, Samuel Coleridge and John Ruskin. Richard Birdsall used the term "American Lake District" in his 1959 overview, *Berkshire County: A Cultural History*.

While the fact is that Berkshire's *hills*, more than its scattered lakes, inspired fiction writers and poets, there indeed grew a circle of influence. "The bloom of these mountains is beyond expression delightful," Herman Melville gushed in *Israel Potter* (1855). Melville was the widest rover of his generation. "He climbed every alluring hill-top, and explored every picturesque corner and hidden nook that he could hear of, or find by seeking," according to J.E.A. Smith. Melville spent a night at the Williams College observatory on Mount Greylock in August 1851.

Sedgwick and Fanny Kemble entertained friends here. Melville and Longfellow had family connections. Hawthorne made an extended country sojourn. Bryant and Stowe visited frequently. This was simultaneous with the rise of an upper class interested in building summer cottages and an industrial-age middle class interested in traveling out of the city and staying at a healthy country place. Consequently, the area's reputation burst.

The adventures of Rip Van Winkle and Ichabod Crane, written by the "Father of American Literature," Washington Irving (1783–1859), inspired Bryant's short stories. In about 1835, Irving visited Stockbridge. "I recall… the thrill of awful interest with which I saw him seated on a sofa in the parlor talking with Miss Sedgwick, and how I vainly tried by the boyish tests at my command, to make out what distinguished him from ordinary gentlemen of quiet dress and manners," Catharine's brother Henry recalled.

Asa Greene (1789–1837) attended Williams College and received his MD from Berkshire Medical Institution in Pittsfield in 1827. He wrote the humorous *Travels in America* (1833) under the name "George Fibbleton," followed the same year by *The Life and Adventures of Dr. Dodimus Duckworth* under his own name. Then came *A Yankee Among the Nullifiers* (1835) as "Elnathan Elmwood Esq."

G.P.R. James farmed as well as wrote while living in Stockbridge. *Library of Congress.*

Londoner George Payne Rainsford James (1799–1860), G.P.R. for short, brought his family across the Atlantic to Stockbridge in 1851. He wrote seven novels, including *The Bride of Landeck* (1878), before moving elsewhere. James was a gentleman farmer and served on the vestry of St. Paul's Church. A friend of Hawthorne's, the author "brought a smoothness to Stockbridge which suggested London drawing rooms," according to Sarah Cabot Sedgwick and Christina Sedgwick Marquand. "He had met Campbell, Southey and Byron and was known to be a friend of Walter Scott's. Urbanely used to success, he took his talent with sophisticated ease and never worked after 11 in the morning. The first draft of his manuscript, which he rarely changed, was dictated to his secretary."

Another Fireside Poet, James Russell Lowell (1819–1891) came here with his family in the summer of 1846, when daughter Blanche needed to recover from a temporary illness. "Stockbridge is without exception the quietest place I was ever in," Lowell wrote a friend. "The postmaster has no regular hours whatever." Longfellow found Lowell "hale as a young farmer."

Transcendentalist Ralph Waldo Emerson (1803–1882) did for essays and poetry what Irving did for fiction: he established an American benchmark. In 1827, the Harvard Divinity School professor visited the Wards and Tappans in north Stockbridge; his daughter Ellen attended Mrs. Sedgwick's Young Ladies' School in Lenox. His verse "The Dome of the Taconics" is a tribute to Mount Everett. Emerson took to the podium to lecture in Lee, Lenox, Great Barrington, Pittsfield and North Adams. Emerson orated at Williams College and wrote in his journal for November 5, 1865:

> *Early in the afternoon Professor* [John] *Bascom carried me in a gig to the top of the West Mountain, and showed me the admirable view down the valley in which this town and Adams lie, with Greylock and his attendant ranges towering in front...Of all tools, an observatory is the most sublime. And these mountains give an inestimable worth to Williamstown and Massachusetts. But, for the mountains, I don't quite like the proximity of a college and its noisy students. To enjoy the hills as a poet, I prefer simple farmers as neighbors.*

Daughter-in-law of Judge Theodore, wife of Charles, sister-in-law of Catharine—all Sedgwicks—and granddaughter of theologian Jonathan Edwards, Elizabeth Buckminster Dwight Sedgwick (1791–1864) had the pedigree to supervise a private Young Ladies' School at her Lenox home from 1828 to 1859. She wrote *Louisa and Her Cousins* (1831), a collection of children's stories, and *A Talk with My Pupils* (1863). One of her scholars at the "character factory," as Sedgwick called it, was Maria Susanna Cummins (1827–1866) of Salem, whose *The Lamplighter* (1854) sold some seventy thousand copies in its first year.

The Hive, the Sedgwick home on Kemble Street, was demolished in 1904 to make way for Spring Lawn, home to Lenox School for Boys from 1926 to 1971.

Eugene Field (1850–1895) attended Williams College. An attempt to make a living as a writer wiped out his inheritance. He took up newspapering and ended up in Chicago, where his "Sharps and Flats" department for the *Record* attained a national following. He was founding editor of the radical magazines *The Masses* and *The Liberator*. Field wrote amusing poetry, including "Wynken, Blynken and Nod" and "Little Boy Blue," both in 1889.

HOLMES'S SEVEN HAPPIEST SUMMERS

Oliver Wendell Holmes Sr. (1809–1894)—who uttered, "There's no tonic like the Housatonic"—studied law. He studied medicine. He wrote essays. He rhymed poetry. He wrote conversational "The Autocrat of the Breakfast-Table" essays for *Atlantic Monthly*. "All through the years of his boyhood and until he succeeded his ancestry in their land possessions in Pittsfield, his parents never failed to make an annual pilgrimage by carriage to this charming spot among the Berkshire hills, in which are what are known as the Canoe Meadows," according to *The Berkshire Hills*.

Oliver Wendell Holmes Sr.'s Canoe Place backed up to the Housatonic River in Pittsfield. Poet Among the Hills, *1895*.

"Seven of the happiest summers of my life were passed in Berkshire with the Housatonic running through my meadows and Greylock looking into my study window," the Fireside Poet said of his home, Canoe Place, on Holmes Road, where he bivouacked from 1848 to 1856. It was Holmes's great-grandfather Jacob Wendell's old farm. Longfellow called it "a snug little place, with views of the river and the mountains."

Among Holmes's compositions identified with the Berkshires are "Poem of Welcome" (Pittsfield Jubilee, 1844), "The Ploughman" (Pittsfield cattle show, 1849), "The Vision" (Housatonic River, 1853) and "The New Eden" (Berkshire

Agricultural Society, 1854). "The Deacon's Masterpiece; or the Wonderful One-Hoss Shay" (1858) described a marvelous two-wheeled, horse-drawn conveyance, each piece carefully crafted to last one hundred years. The novel *Elsie Venner* (1861), set in "Pigwacket Center," was modeled after Pittsfield (particularly South Mountain). It is about the unusual subject of animalization—a human taking on attributes of an animal—in Elsie's case, a rattlesnake.

Expanded by later owners and renamed Holmesdale, Holmes's house is privately owned. Massachusetts Audubon maintains Canoe Meadows. Samuel McKay's shay that inspired the Holmes poem was in the Berkshire Museum from 1914 to 2006, when it was transferred to Ventfort Hall. Justice Oliver Wendell Holmes Jr. gave his father's library to the Berkshire Athenaeum.

LONGFELLOW "FOREVER—NEVER! FOREVER—NEVER!"

Berkshire inspired writers. Hugh C. Wheeler, for example, during the eight months a year he was in Monterey could write sixty to seventy pages a day. "I do some of my best work here," Thornton Wilder said of the Red Lion Inn, which still does hearty business in Stockbridge. There were exceptions. Henry Wadsworth Longfellow admired being in the Berkshires but couldn't work there. "It is difficult to write in this [Pittsfield] house, so closely is it shut in by trees," he journaled in 1846.

Longfellow (1807–1882), modern languages professor at Harvard, married Frances Appleton in 1843. They honeymooned at her family's summer home, Elm Knoll, on East Street in Pittsfield, where Longfellow encountered and poetized "The Clock on the Stairs" (1845).

The author of "Song of Hiawatha" (1855) and "The Midnight Ride of Paul Revere" (1860) made frequent Berkshire visits. In 1846, he boarded at Broadhall, the Melville farm that is now Pittsfield Country Club. He roomed at the Red Lion Inn. He took carriage rides with his father-in-law, Nathaniel Appleton, to North Adams and Williamstown and Greylock. He sipped tea with various Sedgwicks and Lowells and heard Fanny Kemble sing. He wrote in his diary in 1848:

> *We drove to Stockbridge…Passed an hour at the Oxbow* [his father-in-law's land between the Tuckerman and Butler bridges]. *What a lovely place! On three sides shut in by willow and alder hedges and*

Henry Wadsworth Longfellow discovered an interesting clock in Pittsfield. Poet Among the Hills, *1895*.

the flowering wall of the river under the soil, marble enough to build a palace. I build many castles in the air. One of these is on the upland of the Oxbow looking eastward down the valley across this silver bow of the Housatonic.

Longfellow would own eighty acres in Stockbridge himself from 1850 to 1867.

"In Berkshire, Longfellow discovered, as Catharine Sedgwick had found before him and as Holmes would learn later, the fullest and strongest expression of Calvinism, and by adding the contemplated 'spiritual chapter' to *Kavanagh*, he placed it in the tradition of Berkshire novels which had begun with *A New England Tale* and would end with *Elsie Venner*," according to Birdsall. A country romance, *Kavanagh* (1848) includes a character based on Cornelius Mathews (we will meet him in another chapter), who insists American literature be distinctive from European—Longfellow disagreed. The novel anticipates local color writing and contains the first depiction of a lesbian relationship in American literature.

Elm Knoll, popularly called Longfellow House, was razed in 1929 for construction of Pittsfield High School. The front door, fanlight and clock stairway were installed in a replica house built on Crofut Street for Harriet Plunkett. On West Avenue in Great Barrington there is an 1896 replica of Longfellow's Craigie House in Cambridge.

WHERE'S HERMAN MELVILLE'S PIAZZA?

One day in 2005, I telephoned Catherine Reynolds, curator of collections at Arrowhead on Holmes Road in Pittsfield, and threw out the question: "Do you know where Melville's piazza is?"

She didn't hesitate. "Sure, it's just outside the window—"

"No," I interrupted, "where's *Herman's* piazza?"

"Oh, it went to New Jersey to a judge's home somewhere," she said, dashing any hopes that I possessed a rare piece of trivia. I'd come across a newspaper reference to the removal of the original piazza and wondered if the Arrowhead folks were aware of it. Yes, I was comforted to learn, Berkshire Historical Society's institutional memory is remarkably strong—even with several curators and directors over the years. The historical society hadn't even been established when the piazza was taken away.

Herman Melville wrote more than sea tales—he also mused on his Arrowhead chimney and porch. *Library of Congress.*

"I'd love to know what it looks like today," Reynolds said. "I suppose the judge is not still alive."

"Doubt it," I agreed. "The porch was taken away seventy years ago."

The *Berkshire Evening Eagle* headline that had caught my attention, "Piazza of Melville Home Sold to Judge Pitney of New Jersey," was from 1937. The reporter explained that the family living at Arrowhead at the time had struck a deal with Robert Pitney of Mendham, New Jersey.

> *Pitney, a friend of the present owners of the property, Mr. and Mrs. J. Dwight Francis, learned that plans called for tearing down that part of the structure and he expressed a wish that he might have it. A huge van and a force of men from the William Johnson moving firm at Far Hills, N.J., have been in Pittsfield for three days dismantling the porch piece by piece and placing it in a truck for the 200-mile trip.*

Melville had built the open piazza in the 1850s and there, as he took in the Mount Greylock vista and contemplated savage cannibals and demented sea captains, tended young son, Malcolm.

The piazza was removed, Reynolds explained, as the Francises wanted to add on to a wing that had been built since the Melville era. When they rebuilt the porch, it was shorter than in Herman's day. When Arrowhead came into the hands of the historical society in 1975, nearly a century of alterations had to be undone. Obviously not everything could be restored at once, the curator said. The addition was retained, as it contained space for offices and an apartment. But a picture window onto the porch was removed and replaced with period-style windows.

The piazza isn't the only chip of old Arrowhead taken away. Henry A. Murray of Harvard University, principal donor of Melville books and memorabilia to the Melville Room at the Berkshire Athenaeum in Pittsfield, had some planks from the barn, Reynolds said.

A little more needs to be said about the piazza.

Melville found the lack of a porch a major deficiency of the old Thomas Melville farmhouse when he purchased it in 1850: "When I removed into the country," he said in his 1856 short story "The Piazza":

> It was to occupy an old-fashioned farmhouse, which had no piazza—a deficiency the more regretted because not only did I like piazzas, as somehow combining the coziness of indoors with the freedom of outdoors, and it is so pleasant to inspect your thermometer there, but the country round about was such a picture that in berry time no boy climbs hill or crosses vale without coming upon easels planted in every nook, and sunburnt painters painting there. A very paradise of painters. The circle of the stars cut by the circle of the mountains. At least, so looks it from the house; though, once upon the mountains, no circle of them can you see. Had the site been chosen five rods off, this charmed ring would not have been.

So he built a piazza only to be immediately chided by a neighbor who called it a "winter porch," as it was on the shaded side of the house. Perhaps its construction reflected Melville's darker side.

Herman's prose piece, more of a meander than a story with plot or character development, speculates that how one perceives the world depends on one's point of view to begin with, and the better the initial attitude, the better life is. He also puts in a word for the benefits of being able to find new perspectives from standing outside one's circumstance—certainly something in short supply in his mind in his extended, bustling, female-dominated household.

Melville artifacts were frequently placed in odd places and forgotten. An upstairs fireplace, for instance, was uncovered intact in the house in 1977 by Donald G. Smith, Arrowhead director. It was mentioned in a letter Melville wrote to his publisher. Bertine Smith told me her late husband and their youngest daughter, Ruth, bashed through a wall on New Year's Day to reveal the long-hidden feature.

Identified in 1919 among family papers stored in a small trunk by Melville's granddaughter Eleanor Melville Metcalf was the unpublished manuscript of *Billy Budd*.

Melville's great-grandson, Paul Metcalf (1917–1999), poet, novelist, essayist, literary critic and lecturer, located in the attic of his Becket home another trove of Melville family papers and donated them to the Berkshire Athenaeum.

Designated a National Historic Landmark in 1962, Arrowhead is maintained by the Berkshire Historical Society. The Berkshire Athenaeum has a Herman Melville Memorial Room.

Nathaniel Hawthorne's Stockbridge Sojourn

Nathaniel Hawthorne (1804–1864) stagecoached to Pittsfield and its environs for a six-week working vacation in 1838. He described the sojourn in *American Notebooks*:

> *I pointed to a hill at some distance before us, and asked what it was. "That, sir," said he* [a fellow passenger], *"is a very high hill. It is known by the name of Graylock* [sic].*" He seemed to feel that this was a more poetical epithet than Saddleback, which is a more usual name for it. Graylock* [sic], *or Saddleback, is quite a respectable mountain.*

In North Adams, Hawthorne and a companion on September 7 "took a walk by moonlight last evening, on the road that leads over the mountain. Remote from houses, far up on the hillside, we found a lime-kiln, burning near the road; and, approaching it, a watcher started from the ground, where he had been lying at his length. There are several of these lime-kilns in this vicinity."

Hawthorne remembered that kiln when he wrote "Ethan Brand," a story in *The Snow-Image and Other Twice-Told Tales* (1852). The main character resembles a man he met at the North Adams House who had "a large nose—and his face expressed enthusiasm and humor—a sort of smile and twinkle of the eye, with wildness." In the story, lime burner Brand searches for the Unpardonable Sin—which turns out to be within himself.

"The valleys and mountains of the Berkshires had a deeply aesthetic and religious effect upon Hawthorne which, along with the people he met here,

Nathaniel Hawthorne's bust by Jonathan Scott Hartley hovers over the front portico of the Library of Congress in Washington. *Carol Highsmith/Library of Congress.*

lent itself easily to a recurring theme in Hawthorne's works—the struggle of good against evil, the purity of nature against the evil of human beings," Dan Connerton wrote.

In 1849, Hawthorne brought his wife, Sophia (Peabody), and children, Una and Julian, from Salem to the north slope above Lake Mahkeenac. Hawthorne thought he was in Lenox; after all, he went to Lenox for his mail. But the cottage was physically in north Stockbridge.

"At Lenox [*sic*], the air was scented with sweet-grass and clover; and there, in the little red cottage on the lonely farm, Hawthorne had his year of wonders," according to Van Wyck Brooks. "Here Hawthorne wrote *The House of the Seven Gables* [1851] and planned *The Blithedale Romance* [1852], and, while his wife made tracings of Flaxman's outlines on the dull-yellow painted chairs and tables, he told the children stories that explained the drawings, *The Wonder Book, The Tanglewood Tales*." The last two works mention Berkshire locations such as Monument Mountain and Shadow Brook.

Hawthorne wrote despairingly of Berkshire weather in his diary on July 29, 1851: "This is a horrible, horrible, most horrible climate; one knows not, for 10 minutes together, whether he is too cool or too warm; but he is always one or the other; and the constant result is a miserable disturbance of the system. I detest it! I detest it! I de-test it!!!" Though, as Richard Nunley noted, "He wrote this after his second day in the constant company of his five-year-old son, Julian." There emerged a rhythm. While Nathaniel applied pen to paper, Sophia and the tadpoles raised chickens, grew vegetables and explored the countryside.

Sophia Hawthorne liked to socialize; her husband dreaded company. Thus, on one occasion, Nathaniel and son were dispatched homeward while Sophia and daughter visited the Sedgwicks and attended the annual Ice Glen parade. "It looked," Sophia wrote her mother, "as if a host of stars had fallen out of the sky, and broken to pieces."

In the opinion of Walter Prichard Eaton,

> *Hawthorne was a true "solitary," with all the exaggerated shyness of his type. The type is seldom understood by the world at large, and Hawthorne shared the fate of lesser examples, and was generally deemed in Berkshire, according to the contemporary testimony, a morose, unfriendly man...It is recorded that he was so shy that he once climbed over a wall on his way to the Lenox post office, rather than meet a group of pedestrians he saw approaching...However, we had him here once, sixty-four years ago, and here he wrote one of the great novels of our language.*

There were other writing Hawthornes. Julian (1846–1934) became a novelist and biographer. He reminisced of the family stay in Berkshire:

The House of the Seven Gables *must have been going on at this time in the little study; but we knew nothing about that. It is more probable that Herman Melville, who was then writing his great story of* Moby Dick; or, the White Whale, *heard news of the progress of the romance. Melville often would walk over to us from Pittsfield, where he lived, accompanied by a great black Newfoundland dog, on whose back he used to let us ride.*

Youngest daughter, Rose (1851–1926), born in the snuggery in Stockbridge, grew up in Liverpool (when her father was U.S. consul), married George Parsons Lathrop, embraced Roman Catholicism and became a missionary nun. She wrote *Along the Shore* (1888), a collection of verse, and *Memories of Hawthorne* (1897).

The Little Red House where Hawthorne conversed with Kemble, Holmes, Melville, Lowell, E.P. Whipple and G.P.R. James burned in 1890. Cortland Field Bishop installed a marker in 1929. The National Federation of Music Clubs in 1948 built a replica to house music practice rooms for Tanglewood students. Hawthorne's Stockbridge desk is in the Berkshire Museum's collection, the gift of Justice Oliver Wendell Holmes Jr.

FANNY KEMBLE PRESIDED IN LENOX

Born into a theatrical family—her father, Charles, was proprietor of the Covent Garden Theatre in London, and her aunt was the tragedienne Sarah Siddons—Frances Anne Kemble (1809–1893) was a popular stage actress, singer and woman of letters who immigrated to the United States. Her poetry included "To the Young Gentleman About to Graduate from Lenox Academy."

Fanny Kemble—Henry James called her "the terrific Kemble"—learned of the Berkshires through her friend Catharine Sedgwick and first came here in 1832. She returned after her marriage to Philadelphian Pierce Butler disintegrated in 1848. Butler owned cotton plantations in the South. Kemble abhorred slavery. Her *Journal of a Residence on a Georgian Plantation* (1863) was powerful in persuading the British to side with the North during the American Civil War.

Kemble purchased a house on East Street in Lenox in 1851. She called it The Perch.

Kemble "spent part of her summers in Lenox, occasionally coming to Stockbridge and joining in the excursions to Monument Mountain, Perry's Peak, and elsewhere in the neighborhood, of which there was no end," according to Henry Dwight Sedgwick. "She often read Shakespeare on the piazza or in the parlors of Mrs. Charles Sedgwick's house at Lenox for the instruction and pleasure of Mrs. Sedgwick's pupils. Many visitors and villagers, by invitation, gathered round, and were now spell-bound, now electrified, by her wonderful voice as it ran through the gamut of the great master."

Fanny Kemble was a social magnet at The Perch in Lenox. *Johnson Wilson & Co., 1873.*

Her gift of the proceeds of one Shakespeare reading paid for a clock for the Church on the Hill steeple.

She returned to London in 1877. Her novel *Far Away and Long Ago* (1889), written when she was eighty, is set in Lenox and Stockbridge.

The Perch's location on what is now Kemble Street is marked by a bronze plaque and boulder opposite Bellefontaine (Canyon Ranch), placed by neighbor Cortland Field Bishop in 1929, two decades after he demolished the old mansion.

HARRIET BEECHER STOWE FAILED TO AMUSE

Several generations removed, several times renovated, only the spirits remain in the auditorium once known as Julia Sumner Hall—now converted to apartments in the Sumner Block on Great Barrington's Main Street—to

Harriet Beecher Stowe frequently visited her brother in Lenox and her daughter in Stockbridge. *Library of Congress.*

recall the famed speakers whose voices resonated there. Harriet Beecher Stowe's on a Monday evening in October 1872 was one.

Stowe traipsed the lecture circuit late in life. "This is an event that has been brought about by rare good fortune," a *Berkshire Courier* writer said, "and one in which the community will greatly rejoice. Mrs. Stowe appears this season for the first time as a public reader, and like Charles Dickens, she has everywhere drawn thousands of enthusiastic admirers to hear her interpret her own writings."

The community was familiar with Stowe's *Uncle Tom's Cabin*, the most-performed road show in the Berkshires. Stowe wrote the novel about Simon Legree, Little Eva and Topsy in 1852. In no time, there were four traveling stage versions—none authorized, none paying her a royalty. The author's character Uncle Tom is compassionate in the book, stereotyped in the stage play.

The author and her husband, Dr. Calvin Stowe, frequently visited her brother, the Reverend Henry Ward Beecher, in Lenox. A Congregational pastor, Beecher (1813–1887) had acquired Blossom Hill farm in 1853—a gift from Brooklyn friends. He changed the name to Beecher Hill, built a simple dwelling and wrote *Star Papers* here. He dabbled in poetry and later wrote a novel, *Norwood; or Village Life in New England* (1867), set in a town much like Lenox. As other writers before and after, he climbed Mount Greylock.

After Beecher sold his Lenox retreat in 1857, the Stowes visited their daughter Georgiana and her husband, the Reverend Henry Allen, at Laurel Cottage in Stockbridge from 1865 to 1872. Helen Bidwell Lukeman recalled: "One day young [Freeman] Allen was swinging on the gate at the Judge Byington place across the street. A neighbor reprimanded him. He replied,

'I don't care for my neighbor or his ox or his ass, etc.' The person said you must not talk like that. Do you know who said that? 'No' was the reply 'but it sounds like grandma Stowe.'"

The *Courier* hyped Stowe's booking in Great Barrington: "There will undoubtedly be a rush, and the first come will be first served," the editor warned. Special trains were added from north of town and from North Canaan, Connecticut.

"To a majority of her hearers, the entertainment was a success," the *Courier* regretted the next week, "while some were disappointed both in the selections and the reader's power. Mrs. Stowe's efforts as a reader have been rather severely criticized in many places where she has read this fall."

Her Great Barrington experience aside, Stowe in 2007 appeared on a seventy-five-cent U.S. postage stamp.

The Beecher house in Lenox was destroyed in 1893 at the time John Sloane built his new Wyndhurst mansion, today Cranwell Resort. Laurel Cottage in Stockbridge was razed in 1954. Town tennis courts are there today.

ROSE TERRY COOKE AND THE REJECTED MANUSCRIPT

Rose Terry Cooke (1827–1892) by the age of six read a column in *Walker's Dictionary* every day. Her father, a landscape gardener, instilled in her an appreciation of nature. She graduated from the Hartford Female Seminary. After receiving a small inheritance, she gave up teaching in order to write poetry for the *New York Tribune*, *Harper's* and *Atlantic Monthly*.

Cooke "was one of the earliest writers of local-color stories, anticipating Bret Harte by more than a decade," according to Claude M. Simpson.

> *Her tales of New England provincial life, set in her native Connecticut, were popular in the leading periodicals…She wrote one novel, a volume of poems, some juvenile and devotional literature, but her reputation rests on three volumes of stories:* Somebody's Neighbors *(1881),* The Sphinx's Child *(1886), and* Huckleberries Gathered from New England Hills *(1891). She writes with zest and good humor, viewing her odd characters indulgently; yet a streak of iron runs through her make-up and when necessary she deals firmly with stark landscape and narrow meanness of human conduct.*

Rose Terry Cooke of Pittsfield blossomed as a local color writer. *Buffalo Electrotype & Engraving.*

Cooke suffered the travails faced by many writers: rejection. She said in the *Springfield Daily Republican*:

I sent this manuscript with which I myself was pleased to one of our first magazines; they returned it, saying they had all the serials in hand they could use; as my story was only in two parts, not necessarily to be published in two numbers, I perceived at once that this was only a polite excuse. Not daunted I sent it to still another magazine; it came back again with an elaborately polite letter, saying that the canons of taste forbade the editor to accept a story so sad in its motive; that it was a duty to brighten life for the public, not darken it with melancholy detail; so with much regret, etc. etc., it was returned. In the next issue of that magazine there was a ghastly story by [Ivan] Turgenieff, beside which my simple tale of a common New England family was really hilarious…With rather a heavy heart—for I needed the money very much—I tried a third periodical; and the wandering article was to my surprise and delight accepted with such a laudatory letter that I fairly blushed on reading it.

She may be talking about "Freedom Wheeler's Controversy with Providence: A Story of Old New England," which appeared in *Atlantic Monthly* in July 1877.

The wordsmith and her husband, banker and genealogist Rollin Hillyer Cooke of Winsted, Connecticut, moved to Brewster House on East Street, Pittsfield, in 1887. She became incapacitated soon after and stopped writing.

III

ROBBIE BURNS, POIT A TH' GANG WI' AW

Robert Burns (1759–1796) is an important touchstone. English-speaking settlers in North America knew his poetry by heart, and his influence on writers here should not be underestimated.

The Plowman Poet provided muse not only to Holmes (who said, "Burns ought to have passed ten years of his life in America") but also to Longfellow (whose tribute, "Robert Burns," is in Scottish stanza) and Melville (who crafted "Robert Burns: Turning Up a Mouse in Her Nest with the Plough, Nov. 1785"). Emerson, at a Burns festival at Parker House in Boston in 1857, said his vernacular poetry was "the only example in history of a language made classic by the genius of a single man." Hawthorne, when American consul in Great Britain, made a pilgrimage to the bard's birth home in Ayr in 1857 and plucked daisies from a field Burns once plowed. Bryant as a teenager devoured the Scotsman's ballads and was honorary chairman of the Burns Club of the City of New York's Centennial Birthday of Robert Burns gathering at Astor House in 1859. Beecher gave the oration that night.

Josh Billings, who wrote in his own mangling of a Lowland Scots dialect, considered Burns "the *most* Poet that ever lived."

Wallace Bruce, who was born in Hillsdale, New York, of Scottish descent (as if there could be doubt, with a name like that), served as President Benjamin Harrison's American consul in Edinburgh. Bruce recited his own "The Auld Brig's Welcome" at the unveiling of a Burns statue in Ayr in July 1891. The verse appears in *Here's a Hand* (1893), along with an essay, "The Influence of Robert Burns on American Literature."

Ferenc Morton Szasz suggests Burns was America's default national poet well into the nineteenth century because of the many Scots and Scotch-Irish immigrants familiar with the verses, because Burns voiced a cultural independence and linguistic vibrancy and because until Walt Whitman, the United States claimed no native epic poetic voice.

Burns Night participants each January on the poet's birthday yet today gather to consume haggis (a pudding of sheep's organs), tatties (creamed potatoes flavored with nutmeg) or neeps (mashed turnips sweetened with milk and allspice) and toast their glib-penned hero. As the Reverend J.A. Carruth put it in "A Humble Tribute to Robert Burns": "He speaks to Scots; he speaks to a'."

It will take some doing to top the Burns Night held at the Wilson House in North Adams in January 1895. Three hundred people crammed the dining hall to hear Peter MacPhail, a sketch maker for Arnold Print Works, address the haggis in a broad, Gaelic voice—no surprise, as he was born in Mearns, Kincardneshire, Scotland. The *Transcript* reported his words:

> The "Scot abroad" is a phrase not very appropriate when applied to Scotchmen in this beautiful valley of Berkshire; for here he is very much at home. When he views for the first time the majestic beauty of the Berkshire hills, the salutation of William Tell rises instinctively to his lips "ye crags and peaks, I'm with you once again." To some the Hoosac range will suggest the Peltland, Ochil, Grampian hills or Campsie Fells. To others again Greylock will suggest Ben Lomond, Ben Ledi, Ben Nevis or Cruachen Ben. In imagination he can cloth[e] them with purple heather and brawling brooks, with tartan plaids and white cockades, with kilts and hose, highland bag pipes, filabeg and sporan.

IV
WRITERS AT THEIR PEAKS

HENRY DAVID THOREAU SCALED MOUNT GREYLOCK AND MOUNT EVERETT

Henry David Thoreau (1817–1862), the Concord naturalist, poet, teacher, pencil maker and surveyor, spread nuggets of wisdom with the glee of Johnny Appleseed. In *Walden* (1854), he speaks of a universal ownership of the mountains and streams: "I retained the landscape, and I have since annually carried off what it yielded without a wheelbarrow."

Thoreau visited Saddleback Mountain, now known as Mount Greylock, in July 1844. He wrote about his chilly night beneath a wooden Williams College observation tower in *A Week on the Concord and Merrimack Rivers* (1849).

He descended to Pittsfield and continued to the Catskills. J. Parker Huber wrote:

> *Thoreau and* [walking companion and poet William Ellery] *Channing returned via Bash Bish Falls in southwestern Massachusetts, again over the Berkshires and through the villages of Mount Washington and Chester. Likely they passed, and at least viewed, Monument Mountain, in the towns of Stockbridge and Great Barrington, the meeting place of Melville and Hawthorne on 5 August 1850. At Chester they took the railroad east, arriving in Concord on August 1.*

Henry David Thoreau spent a chilly night on Mount Greylock. *Maxham Daguerreotype 1856/ Thoreau Institute at Walden Woods.*

Thoreau's woods buddy Channing (1818–1901), who had stayed at the Berkshire Coffee-House in Lenox in 1842, made notes in his copy of *A Week* to confirm the path.

And there's other evidence of their route.

While building a cabin on the shore of an outlying pond in Concord in 1845, Thoreau couldn't shake from his head a vivid recollection of a small mountain pond he had seen the summer before. "A tarn high up on the side of a mountain, its bottom far above the surface of other lakes," he said in *Walden*.

That inspirational body is surely Guilder Pond in Mount Washington. A rounded ledge protrudes from the shore into the irregularly shaped pond. It is surrounded by gently sloping, mostly coniferous forest. Today, water dribbles over a spillway into Guilder Brook. There is no distant view; looking in any direction but the southwest (where Mount Everett rises), it seems to hover near the clouds.

No wonder the tarn stuck in Thoreau's mind.

Edward Hitchcock of Amherst College, conducting an official geological survey of Massachusetts in 1837–39, gushed about Bash Bish Falls. Thoreau owned a copy of Hitchcock's book and sought out Bash Bish Falls to see for himself.

Albert Nash of Falls Village, Connecticut, made an excursion to Bash Bish Falls in 1846 and wrote about it for the *Housatonic Mirror*: "This is *the* gorge, the ravine above scarcely being remembered or noticed."

Thoreau in his journal in May 1851 was still thinking about that mountain lake: "I had in my mind's eye a silent gray tarn which I had seen the summer before high up the side of a mountain, Bald Mountain."

Nash tied it together: "We call it [the highest peak in Mount Washington] Mount Everett because that is the name given it by Mr. Hitchcock…This peak is however more generally know[n] by the name of Ball, or Bald mountain."

His trek through these parts was transformative for Thoreau, emboldening him to begin his Walden experiment.

Remarkably, immediately after Thoreau's visit, and surely with no knowledge of it, David Dudley Field Jr. (1805–1894) of Stockbridge, sparked by a comment by childhood friend and Williams College president Mark Hopkins at the Berkshire Jubilee held in Pittsfield on August 22 and 23, 1844, within days traveled the length of Berkshire County by wagon. Starting from Mount Greylock, which he summited with a driver the evening before, in order to witness sunrise, he ended at The Dome in Mount Washington, passing through Pittsfield along the way—all places Thoreau also visited!

"The ascent was fatiguing enough to make us sleep soundly, though our eagerness brought us up the next morning by daybreak, that we might see the sun rise," Field wrote in the *Democratic Review*. They descended to the Williamstown valley and, after thirteen hours and fifty miles, made their way to Eagle's Nest above Bash Bish Falls. "Here we stood, looking at the long blue line of mountain, as the sun went down behind it, and so ended our 'journey of a day.'"

The excursion affirms Field's love of outdoors and the freedom to roam—as we will see next.

Bash Bish Falls State Park and Mount Everett State Reservation in Mount Washington are open to the public, as is Mount Greylock Reservation in North Berkshire. There's a replica of Thoreau's Walden cabin in the woods behind Berkshire School in Sheffield, built by students under English teacher (and poet) Hilary Russell's direction in 2003. There are regular July reenactments of Thoreau's Greylock climb. Lauren R. Stevens is a frequent leader.

Mrs. Fields and Miss Field Kept Pace on the Monument Mountain Picnic

A ramble up Monument Mountain in Great Barrington on August 5, 1850, marked the first Herman Melville and Nathaniel Hawthorne handshake. Hawthorne was grateful for Melville's positive comments in *Literary World* on his writing. Melville was thrilled to find a soul mate.

A half dozen participants wrote all-too-brief accounts of the picnic. Later historians, biographers and trail guides almost universally exaggerate what went on, miss details or simply get things wrong. The picnic party did not take refuge from the rain in a *cave*, for example. Publisher Evert A. Duyckinck (1816–1878) wrote to his wife it was "a few feet of rock with a damp underground of mosses and decay." It was a western overhang on Squaw Peak.

And it wasn't a stag affair. Two young women kept pace with the literary luminaries who strode up the narrow trail that day.

Hawthorne's publisher, James T. Fields (1817–1881) of the Boston firm Tichnor & Fields, wasn't about to abandon his new bride, "the violet of the season in Berkshire," as fellow hiker Cornelius Mathews described her. Mrs. Fields was the former Eliza Willard. Theirs was a happy union but one ordained not to last. Eliza in July learned she had tuberculosis. Seeking a change of venue, the Fieldses traveled to the Berkshires to visit the Hawthornes. They were included when David Dudley Field Jr. assembled his uphill amble. Duyckinck said Field "has cut out for us all…the celebrities of Stockbridge."

Field was a prolific writer of legal code—and at least one poem about Mount Greylock. His brother Henry noted Dudley "was always getting up excursions to Monument Mountain." This one was prompted by a chance encounter with Duyckinck and Mathews on the train from New York. Field had contributed to *Democratic Review*, of which Duyckinck was literary editor. The *Review* was a voice of the Young Americans cultural and political movement.

Cresting the 742-foot rise was arduous, but Eliza Fields enjoyed the outing. "My little miss is well," her husband wrote to a friend. The second female in the party, Jeanie Lucinda Field, was Dudley's seventeen-year-old daughter. The family was a distinguished one; besides Uncle Henry, a clergyman and writer, Uncle Stephen was a Supreme Court justice and Uncle Cyrus placed the first Atlantic cable. When in a few years Jeanie met Cyrus's friend Sir Anthony Musgrave, colonial governor of British Columbia, she fell in love and married him.

Oliver Wendell Holmes Sr. was tickled to join the gathering, as was nonscribbler Henry Dwight Sedgwick II, who had already topped the mountain in stride with James Russell Lowell four years earlier.

Fields recalled, "We scrambled to the top with great spirit, and when we arrived, Melville, I remember, bestrode a peaked rock, which ran out like a bowsprit, and pulled and hauled imaginary ropes for our delectation."

Duyckinck added, "Dr. Holmes peeped about the cliffs and protested it affected him like ipecac. Hawthorne looked wildly about for the great carbuncle. Mathews read Bryant's poem. The exercise was glorious."

Mathews (1817–1889), the unrepentant comic, novelist and giddy Young American, assigned participants odd names in his account in *Literary World*. "Noble Melancholy," as he called Hawthorne, was "a delightful mystical essayist." "New Neptune," aka Melville, was "the sea-dog of our Berkshire homestead." "Town Wit," or Holmes, was a participant "whose verses and jeux d'esprit are on everybody's tongue."

Cornelius Mathews wrote a curious but fascinating account of the 1850 Monument Mountain picnic. *Library of Congress.*

The picnickers knew each other better than you might suspect. Duyckinck was a leading advocate for a new New York City–based American literature. Though he rose through the old school, Bryant occasionally wrote for Duyckinck's publication. Melville and Hawthorne did too, even though the *Review* credited *Typee* to "Sherman Melville," and Duyckinck wildly compared Hawthorne to "the rough hairy rind of the cocoa-nut enclosing its sweet whiteness." Lawyer Field's thrust for the Young Americans was the signification recodification of the common law—to establish rules, rather than rely on precedent, as was the English method.

The group returned to Field's Laurel Cottage on Main Street, Stockbridge, for munchies—the conversation certainly about literary matters. Bostonians Holmes and Fields were outnumbered, if not outwitted, by the Big Apple energizers even further when another Young American, former Stockbridge clergyman, now travel writer, Joel T. Headley (1813–1897), arrived to wade the group across the Housatonic River to explore dark Ice Glen, which Dudley Field owned.

"Everything about the picnic was highly symbolic," literary historian Edward L. Widmer wrote. Though, "for all the attention the outing has received, our understanding of it is still incomplete."

Melville and Hawthorne didn't talk much that day, but they soon forged a friendship—one that had a particular influence on the former's work-in-progress, *The Whale*. "After supper," Hawthorne related of one summer evening in 1851, "Melville and I had a talk about time and eternity, things of this world and next, and books, and publishers, and all possible and impossible matters, that lasted pretty deep into the night."

Monument Mountain Reservation is a property of the Trustees of Reservations. Each August, the literary picnic is re-created under the auspices of the Berkshire Historical Society. Gordon Hyatt has led the walks for a quarter century. Someone reads Bryant's "Monument Mountain," about an ill-fated Indian maiden, and all salute the poet with nonalcoholic champagne. Ice Glen is owned by Laurel Hill Association.

THE QUILLDRIVING GOODALES OF MOUNT WASHINGTON

Sisters Elaine (1863–1953) and Dora Read (1866–1953) Goodale, born at Sky Farm in Mount Washington, were the daughters of Henry Sterling Goodale (1836–1906) and his wife, Deborah "Dora" Read Hill Goodale (1839–1910). Remarkably, all of these Goodales, plus another daughter, Rose Sterling (1870–1965), wrote for publication.

Henry was from Egremont stock, a country boy with country ways, though not uneducated. His wife was from faded but distinguished Connecticut lineage. She had a classic education and home-educated her children. Elaine and Dora Read were inseparable in their remote domain, overlooking the potato field one still encounters in driving to the mountaintop from South Egremont.

Elaine's first published verse was "Papa's Birth-Day" in the *Berkshire Courier* for June 12, 1872. The poem was signed simply "Elaine" and was subtitled "Written by a Poetess Only Eight Years Old." Excited about his daughters' wordcraft, Henry submitted their poems to the children's magazine *St. Nicholas*, and several appeared in the December 1877 issue.

"Our education was overwhelmingly literary and humanistic," Elaine wrote in *Sister to the Sioux*. "I was introduced to Shakespeare at the age of eleven and not long after to *The Marble Faun*, *The Mill on the Floss*, and *David Copperfield*—each a milestone! Long winter evenings are remembered in association with Gibbon and Macaulay."

Jaws dropped in 1878 when G.P. Putnam's published *Apple-Blossoms: Verses of Two Children* and it immediately sold out. The sisters had more rhymes in stock, and *In Berkshire With Wild Flowers* came out in 1879. Elaine published *Journal of a Farmer's Daughter* (1881) solo. Dora published verse in *Harper's*, and later collections included *Heralds of Easter* (1897) and *Mountain Dooryards* (1946).

Henry refused reporters access for interviews with the girls and did his best to keep fans at bay. He was not unfamiliar with the world of publishing. His comical verse "Does Farming Pay?" was in *Harper's* in October 1880, and he offered forty-five-minute recitations on the subject.

Royalties from the sisters' books maintained the family for a few years, but eventually the marriage crumbled. Henry had unbounding love for his daughters and an uncontainable enthusiasm for everything but serious farming. He moved to New York City to manage a hotel. Elaine went to Hampton Institute, taught at an Indian school and married a Sioux man, Dr. Charles A. Eastman. Mrs. Goodale and the other children moved to Connecticut. Dora Read never married. The last child at home, she assumed the care of her mother. The two wrote for *Harper's* and the *Christian*

Elaine Goodale of Mount Washington was a professional writer from age fourteen. Growing up at Sky Farm, she and her younger sister Dora Read Goodale wrote loving verses about flowers and family. Apple-Blossoms, *1878*.

Union. In 1929, Dora Read moved to Tennessee, where she assisted in a medical mission to the underprivileged. Sister Rose married Redington M. Dayton and lived in Connecticut. Some of her verses appeared in Christian periodicals. Brother Robert (1877–1957), a lawyer, confined his writing to legal opinions.

If ever there's testimony to a mountain's nurturing power on a family, it's the Goodales and Mount Washington.

The Goodale homestead—neither dwelling nor barn survives—is part of Mount Everett State Reservation.

V
AND THE WORDS FLOW

NOVELISTS

There are lots of ways to arrange books on a shelf. Let's put novelists together by community.

Alford

Known for his Wessex novels, Englishman John Cowper Powys (1872–1963) found respite from his travels and lectures on a farm he owned here from 1929 to 1934. His novels include *A Glastonbury Romance* (1933) and *Weymouth Sands* (1934). He later moved to South Wales.

Laura Chester (b. 1949) has written more than a dozen volumes of poetry, short stories, fiction and nonfiction since 1972, including *Bitches Ride Alone* (1991), *The Story of the Lake* (1995) and *Rancho Weirdo* (2008). *Hiding Glory* (2007) is a children's book. She defies being placed in a niche, she told me in 1992. "Think of it as a closet of clothes. They all fit you, but they're all different."

Great Barrington

Two men who achieved fame under other names just…dropped in.

Born Teodor Jozef Konrad Korzeniowski (1857–1924), the Polish novelist changed his name to Joseph Conrad when he became a naturalized British subject in 1886. His writings include *Heart of Darkness* (1899), *Lord Jim* (1900) and *The Secret Agent* (1907). Touring America in 1923, Conrad was guest of Mr. and Mrs. Elbridge Adams at Green River Farm on West Sheffield Road. Conrad signed books in bibliophile Adams's extensive collection. (Adams published *Joseph Conrad: The Man* in 1952.)

According to Walter Prichard Eaton:

> *He was a charming guest, Adams recorded, always ready for a chat or some music or whatever was suggested, except a walk or anything requiring physical exertion. The local newspapers would have it that he made pious pilgrimages to the homes or the haunts of Herman Melville, William Cullen Bryant and other literary celebrities. As a matter of fact he never stirred farther from the house than the front terrace, to get the view of Mt. Everett to the southwest, or of Tom Ball to the north, the latter having as he thought a distinctly Italian aspect.*

A later owner of the house showed me a drypoint print of Conrad listening to Brahms, made by Scots artist Sir Muirhead Bone during the writer's two-night stay. It was framed and hanging in the music room.

Making an even shorter visit, Cadet A.J. Horowitz (b. 1925), flying out of Stewart Field, West Point, in May 1945, ran out of fuel in his AT-6 trainer. Through fog and darkness, he sought a clearing for an emergency landing. He crashed nose down right beside a house on Cottage Street. There was no explosion. Unscathed, he went on to become an award-winning author under the name James Salter. His first novel was *The Hunters* (1958). *Dusk and Other Stories* (1988) won a PEN/Faulkner Award. *All That Is* and *Collected Stories* came out in 2013.

Concert violinist Albert Spalding (1888–1953) called his summer residence Aston Magna, after a favorite place in Gloucestershire in the Cotswolds. His novel *A Fiddle, A Sword, A Lady* (1953), issued under his true name, is about Giuseppe Tartini, an eighteenth-century violinist, composer and swordsman.

Emmanuel Dongala (b. 1941), who teaches at Simon's Rock College, relates a coming-of-age story set in a village in Congo Republic—where he grew up—in *Little Boys Come from the Stars* (2001). He won the Cezam Prix Littéraire Inter CE for *Johnny Chién Merchant* in 2004.

Lee

Lucy Ellen Guernsey's novel *Grandmother Brown's School Days* (1875) is set in Lee and Beartown. Guernsey (1826–1899) edited *Parish Visitor* for distribution in homes, hospitals and prisons. Most of her more than sixty books were for the American Sunday School Union.

Lenox

Nancy Goldstone's *Bad Business* (1991) is a satirical take on advertising, government and Wall Street. Among writings by her husband, Lawrence Goldstone, is *Rights* (1992), whose characters include a homeless man fighting for his right to loiter.

Goldsmith Richard W. Wise turned his hand to writing with *The French Blue* (2009), a historical novel about seventeenth-century French gem merchant Jean-Baptiste Tavernier.

Mount Washington

Pulitzer Prize–winning novelist (for *Andersonville* in 1956) MacKinlay Kantor (1904–1977) was a scenario writer, war correspondent and technical consultant for the U.S. Air Force. In Mount Washington, where he and his wife, Irene, rented a cottage on Salisbury Road for three summers in the early 1970s, the writer was known as "Mack." Robert L. Austin recalled, "He was a great raconteur who loved to sing and play the guitar."

North Adams

Bradford Smith (1909–1964) worked for the foreign branch of the Office of War Information in Washington during World War II. He published *To the Mountain* (1936) while living in Tokyo. Another novel, *The Arms Are Fair* (1943), is a sensitive depiction of a Japanese soldier, written while he was teaching at Columbia University.

Pittsfield

William Stearns Davis (1877–1930) was the son of the Reverend William V. Davis, a pastor of First Church. He wrote *Belshazzar: A Tale of the Fall of Babylon* (1902); *A Victor of Salamis* (1907); *The Beauty of the Purple* (1924); *Gilman of Redford, a Friend of Caesar* (1927); and other historical novels.

Michael J. Fox starred in the film version of one-time Pittsfield resident Jay McInerney's *Bright Lights, Big City*. The book came out in 1984, chronicling the on-the-edge lifestyle of a young man working in a major New York magazine's fact-checking department. The writer was born in Hartford, Connecticut, in 1955. The son of a Crane & Co. vice-president, McInerney graduated from Taconic High School in Pittsfield in 1972 and was a 1976 cum laude graduate of Williams College. He was a fact checker for the *New Yorker* before writing full time. Later works include *Ransom* (1985) and *The Last of the Savages* (1996).

Born in New York City, Cynthia Propper Seton (1926–1982) wrote a column for the *Berkshire Eagle* when she lived here. Her novels include *The Half-Sisters* (1974) and *A Fine Romance* (1976). The last was nominated for a National Book Award. Her final novel was *A Private Life* (1982).

Sandisfield

Journalist and freelance writer Miriam Karmel features a sweet, widowed, arthritic, eighty-five-year-old protagonist in the novel *Being Esther* (2013).

Sheffield

Mrs. L.D. Shears, writing as F.E. Ware, incorporated Sheffield people and settings in her third novel, *Little Brown Bessie* (1877). According to the introduction, "In a New England village, the author of the following narrative was born and reared. The scenes and incidents pictured here are not sketches from the imagination, but actual occurrences." The background is the imaginary town of Alderly, where John Dikeman and his wife, Sally, live a marriage of disappointment. Their daughter, Bessie, flees to the city.

Hal Borland (1900–1978) and his wife, Barbara Dodge Borland, owned a mountainside farm south of Bartholomew's Cobble, in a section of

Salisbury known as Weatogue. Borland wrote a nature column for the *New York Times* and the *Berkshire Eagle*. He wrote nature and dog books and novels including *When Legends Die* (1963), about a young Ute Indian trying to live in the old way.

Stockbridge

"There's no violence, no anger, no meanness, no speed, no changes," Hollis Hodges (1920–2004) told me of his novel *Norman Rockwell's Greatest Painting* (1988). The story is about Ebert Olney, a widower, and Mary Ostrowski, a widow. Olney's home in the book appears to be across the street from the former Rockwell residence. A Rockwell painting, the author admitted, is something of a gimmick in the book—a reason to bring the characters together. Hodges's earlier novels *The Fabricator* (1978) and *Don't Tell Me Your Name* (1981) were made into movies. Hodges moved to Stockbridge in 1962. He was a social worker in the state Department of Public Welfare in Pittsfield for a dozen years.

West Stockbridge

Teo Savory (1907–1989) won a Massachusetts Council on the Arts and Humanities Award in 1979 for *Stonecrop: The Country I Remember*, an episodic novel about unusual characters in West Stockbridge, where she lived. The writer was born in Hong Kong, educated in Paris and London and divided her time between theatrical endeavors in New York City and a country house in Freedleyville here.

Williamstown

Robb Forman Dew (b. 1946) won the 1983 American Book Award for best novel for her first work, *Dale Loves Sophie to Death*. She earned a Guggenheim Foundation grant. Her second novel was *The Time of Her Life* (1984). *Fortunate Lives* (1993) brought the writer back to the characters of her first book: Martin Howells, his wife and eighteen-year-old son. Howells is a professor at a college in "West Bradford." But the settings, there's little doubt, are Williamstown, North Adams and Tanglewood. The Berkshires have inspired her writing. "For me it's crucial. I didn't write well until we moved here," she told Lesley Ann Beck in 2002.

National Book Award nominee Jim Shepard (b. 1956) counts among his books *Love and Hydrogen: New and Selected Stories* (2004) and *Project X* (2005). He has taught at Williams College.

Michael C. Quadland grew up in Williamstown. In private psychotherapy practice, he has taught human sexuality at Mt. Sinai School of Medicine in New York City. He was a founder of Gay Men's Health Crisis. *That Was Then* (2008) is about the effect of adolescent confusion on adult lives.

H.H. BALLARD'S MASONIC NOVEL

Harlan Hoge Ballard, librarian for the Berkshire Athenaeum in Pittsfield for nearly five decades, wrote one of the more unusual Berkshire literary works—a Masonic novel.

Ballard (1853–1934) studied at Williams College and for six years was Lenox High School principal. He wrote *Handbook of Blunders Designed to Prevent 1,000 Common Blunders in Writing and Speaking* (1885). Keenly interested in the study of natural science, in 1875 he established the Agassiz Association to promote science and education.

Even after he joined the Berkshire Athenaeum in Pittsfield in 1887, Ballard was a busy writer with *The World of Matter* (1892), a guide to chemistry and mineralogy, and three Barnes' Readers for schoolchildren (1883). Though he long toiled on a translation of Virgil's *Aeneid* (1902–11), his best-known work was *Adventures of a Librarian* (1929).

Ballard, who married Lucy Bishop Pike of Lenox in 1879, was active with the Berkshire Historical and Scientific Society. He joined Crescent Lodge, Ancient Free and Accepted Masons in 1888 and was twice the lodge's master. He also belonged to Royal Arch Masons, Knights Templar and the Lodge of Perfection.

Ballard became a thirty-third-degree Mason in 1929, the order's highest level—and he couldn't contain his enthusiasm. He wrote a novel stressing the fraternal organization's merits.

The Tiler's Jewel (1921) story is this: Helen Prindle's father has died and left no insurance. She and her mother and younger brother are forced to move into a small apartment near South Market in Boston and subsist on sewing jobs and Jimmy's earnings peddling newspapers. It is September 1919, and the police are about to strike.

Mrs. Prindle, coming across her husband's gold tiler's jewel, scoffs. "'Just some of Father's foolish Mason secrets, I suppose,' sighed Mrs. Prindle. 'He spent more money for dues and suppers than would have kept us for a year. Good land! I presume he paid thirty or forty dollars for this thing! I tried my best to keep him from joining, but it didn't do any good.'"

A fellow craftsman comes to the rescue. The lodge had taken up a collection after Prindle's death but couldn't locate the widow, as she had moved. Learning more about her father's Masonic work in helping widows and children, Helen conceives a bold plan. She wants Mother's Day re-designated as Mothers' and Widows Week and all church collections dedicated to charity for those Sundays.

The Berkshire Athenaeum maintains a Berkshire Authors Room and a Herman Melville Room, as well as an extensive collection of Berkshire history and genealogical materials. It has original manuscripts by Rose Terry Cooke and scores and scripts by Liddle and Boltwood.

EDITH WHARTON'S MOTORING ADVENTURES

Charles Cook of East Lee steered a black Pope-Hartford to Mount Greylock's crest in 1904, the first gasoline-powered vehicle to do so. It was two years after a pair of steam-powered Locomobiles had quietly rolled to the peak.

But the Locomobiles didn't have Edith Wharton in the passenger seat.

Edith Newbold Jones Wharton (1862–1937), the first woman to win the Pulitzer Prize for Literature, traveled to Berkshire's remote corners. According to Miriam Levine, she

> *visited Lenox in 1899 and, two years later, bought 113 acres on the southwestern edge of town for $40,600. The land's highest point sloped through meadows and woods to the shore of Laurel Lake. Wharton was born into a well-to-do New York City family. She and her husband, Edward (Teddy), lived at Newport, New York and France as well as Lenox. She enjoyed a wide readership with* The House of Mirth *(1905) and other novels.*
>
> *With the income from trust funds and an inheritance of $500,000, Edith Wharton was free to create a magnificent house. Professional success gave her confidence. Like her writing,* The Mount *was her creation. She chose the site, design and decoration.*

Edith Wharton of Lenox was the first woman to win the Pulitzer Prize for Literature. *Library of Congress.*

After she left for Europe in 1911, Wharton wrote two books that made rich use of Berkshire settings: *Ethan Frome* (1911) and *Summer* (1917). Wharton said in her autobiography that the books "were the result of explorations among villages still bedrowned in a decaying rural existence."

Frome is set in "Starkfield," where residents read the *Bettsbridge Eagle.* Frome leads a mundane, frustrating life caring for his invalid wife. He flirts with his wife's cousin, Mattie. They make a suicide pact and sled down a steep hill and into a tree. Wharton capitalized on a sledding accident that actually happened, on March 11, 1904, at the foot of Courthouse Hill in Lenox.

McClure's magazine serialized *Summer* in 1917. The sensual novel's heroine, Charity Royall, a country gal new to village social life, spurns her widowed adoptive father's offer of marriage and has an affair with a city man. She struggles with her rustic family origins and with where she wants to go with her life. Where did Wharton find inspiration for Charity's mountain people?

"I may mention that every detail about the colony of drunken mountain outlaws described in 'Summer' was given to me by the rector of the church at Lenox (near which we lived), and that the lonely peak I have called 'the Mountain' was in reality Bear Mountain, an isolated summit not more than twelve miles from our own home," Wharton wrote in *A Backward Glance.*

> *The rector had been fetched there by one of the mountain outlaws to read the Burial Service over a woman of evil reputation; and when he arrived every one in the house of mourning was drunk, and the service was performed as*

I have related it….Needless to say, when "Summer" appeared, this chapter was received with indignant denial by many reviewers and readers; and not the least vociferous were the New Englanders who had for years sought the reflection of local life in the rose-and-lavender pages of their favourite authoresses—and had forgotten to look into Hawthorne's.

Wharton's friend Henry James Jr. (1843–1916) summered here to complete a travel book called *The American Scene* (1905). Among his fictions are *A Portrait of a Lady* (1880) and *The Bostonians* (1886). He wrote in 1904: "This exquisite Indian summer day sleeps upon these really admirable little Massachusetts mountains, lakes and woods, in a way that lulls my perpetual sense of precipitation…It is all very interesting and quite unexpectedly and almost uncannily delightful."

James admired Wharton's Springfield-made runabout, paid for by her book royalties, royalties that far outdistanced his own. During the heat of the Lenox summer, James and Wharton motored "daily, incessantly, over miles and miles of lustrous landscape lying motionless under the still glaze of heat. While we were moving he was refreshed and happy, his spirits rose, the twinkle returned to his lips and eyes," Wharton observed in *A Backward Glance*.

The Mount is a National Historic Landmark. Its collection includes Wharton's personal library.

WILLIAM DEAN HOWELLS'S QUIET SUMMER

William Dean Howells (1837–1920), the "father of American realism," was best known for *The Rise of Silas Lapham* (1885), the study of a hard-driven American businessman.

Howells had a long career as a journalist and editor. He struck a spark with a best-selling campaign biography of Abraham Lincoln, which led to his plum appointment as American consul in Venice during the Civil War. He married Elinor Mead in 1862, and they raised two daughters and one son.

Upon his return from Italy, Howells became an editor of the *Atlantic Monthly*. Howells asserted the merits of American realist fiction with an essay for the *Century* in which he defended the writing of Henry James.

Howells wrote to his friend Sam Clemens on June 6, 1885: "As soon as we are settled in the Berkshire House, Great Barrington, Mass., where we go on Monday, my wife will write and tell her [Mrs. Clemens] how sorry we

William Dean Howells brought his daughter to Great Barrington for alternative medical treatment. *Library of Congress.*

were not to come at her invitation or your repetition of it. We expect to be at G.B. a month."

There were temptations to travel, even an offer to meet James Russell Lowell in Boston, but the writer resisted. What was he doing in Great Barrington that Howells would pass up such invitations?

Turns out his oldest daughter, Winifred, suffered from an apparent nervous disorder. Apparent, because that wasn't her actual ailment, and the misdiagnosis would lead to her premature death in 1889 at age twenty-six.

The Howellses were in Great Barrington for Winifred's respite. A mineral spring had recently been discovered at the Hopkins quarry on Quarry Street.

The summer visit to Great Barrington ended on a high note as far as Howells's fortunes were concerned. He landed a juicy assignment writing the "Editor's Study" column for *Harper's New Monthly Magazine*, for $3,000 a year, plus $10,000 for a new novel.

Howells became increasingly political. He opposed the Spanish-American War. He helped found the National Association for the Advancement of Colored People. He wrote and wrote. But try to find one of his books today.

Walter Prichard Eaton Sprouted a Back-to-the-Country Movement

Walter Prichard Eaton (1878–1957) went to work for the *Boston Journal* immediately after graduating from Harvard in 1900. From there he leapt to New York to join the *Tribune*'s theater department. He was drama critic for *American Magazine* until 1918.

Eaton discovered the Berkshires in the early 1900s, following his marriage to Elise Morris Underhill. They settled in Stockbridge in 1910, renting a house on Main Street from Brown Caldwell, part of the old Jonathan Edwards place. Eaton edited the *Stockbridge Magazine* in 1914–15. His *The Bird-House Man* (1916), set in "Southmead," short for Stockbridge, is a light romance about Ruth Barnes, who, at the urging of father-surrogate Alec Farnum, the man of the title, reluctantly agrees to pose for a portrait by the young artist Robert Eliot.

The Eatons moved to Sheffield in 1917, to an 1829 brick dwelling on Undermountain Road that could have been—but wasn't—the one described in his novel *The Idyl of Twin Fires* (1914). That book helped inspire a back-to-the-country movement.

"I wrote *The Idyl of Twin Fires* long before I owned a house or even expected to own one," Eaton said in the *Boston Transcript*. "I wrote it for the same reason Dr. Johnson declared all authors write books—to earn money."

Eaton admitted that his "little story of the rehabilitation of an old house and the revolt to the country living of a man and woman" was "a bit immoral even then, and is now quite hopelessly so." He explained in an introduction to a second edition in 1924 that fixing up a tumbling house and pruning a decrepit orchard were inexpensive and easy to do—from "sitting in my study chair in Stockbridge, where the book was written. But it was so costly, and so incredibly toilsome, to do them actually!"

Walter Prichard Eaton spurred a back-to-the-country movement with his novel. *Author's collection.*

When the Eatons decided to try it for real, he went on, "we bought this old brick house in Sheffield, under the mountain…and purchased 200 acres…We remodeled in war time, and so rapidly did our money disappear that we used up not only the proceeds of the book in which the structure was immortalized, but a lot more besides, and even now the house isn't finished."

Eaton headed Yale University's drama department from 1933 until 1947. He wrote *The Purple Door Knob* and other one-act plays. He was a columnist for the *Berkshire Eagle*. Among his collections of his nature essays was *In Berkshire Fields* (1920). He was an enthusiastic advocate of the Appalachian Trail, constructed in the 1920s.

Quite simply, he was in love with the country. *Twin Fires is privately owned today.*

FINNISH MAID SALLY SALMINEN WROTE A NOVEL

A Scandinavian maid in the Rodney Procter residence Orleton Farms in Stockbridge finished writing what would become a prize-winning novel, *Katrina*, in 1936. It wasn't an upstairs-downstairs kind of novel; it was about the fishing community in her homeland, Vargata, Vårdö, on the Åland Islands of Finland. People in Åland speak mainly Swedish.

Daughter of a Swedish mother and Finnish father, Sally Alina Ingeborg Salminen (1906–1976) attended public elementary school, worked in a country grocery and then moved to Sweden to work as a domestic and clerk in a bakery and study correspondence and bookkeeping. "I had to take Swedish language and spelling in those courses," she told the *Berkshire Eagle*. "The lessons taught me to look things up for myself."

She and her sister Aili came to the United States in 1930 "to get out and see something of the world. I wanted to go some place."

While in the employ of the Procters at their Park Avenue apartment, Salminen wrote in her spare time. She entered the manuscript in a contest sponsored by a Swedish-Finnish publishing house, Holge Schildts Förlag, and won the first prize for best novel written in Swedish: $1,100 and publication.

The writer explained the main economy of Vårdö was fishing, "and it falls on the lot of the women to do most of the hard work on the farms when the men are away," the *Eagle* said. "Her father…owned a farm on Vårdö and was the mail carrier, who in his small boat ferried the mails from one island to another. The young author helped her mother and her 11 brothers and sisters with the farm work, rising in the cold Arctic dawn to milk the cows, feed the chickens and pigs, cut the hay and harvest the potatoes."

Katrina was translated into twenty languages. Farrar & Rinehart published an English translation in 1937.

Salminen used part of her winnings to return to her homeland and in 1940 married Danish painter Johannes Dürhkopf. They lived in Denmark, and the author continued to write, though none of her ten later prose works

Prize-winning novelist Sally Salminen was a maid at Orleton Farms in Stockbridge in the 1930s. *Åland postage stamp, 1996.*

was as popular as the first. She also wrote travel books and a memoir, *Sally's Saga* (1968). She was featured in a 1945 documentary film, *Sally Salminen*.

Salminen's image appeared on a 2.80-mark Europa Åland commemorative postage stamp in 1996.

The Orleton horse farm has other owners today.

SIGRID UNDSET, MONTEREY'S NORWEGIAN FICTIONIST

As wonderful a way as she had with words—she won the Nobel Prize for Literature in 1928, after all—Sigrid Undset (1882–1949) was less than articulate about the world situation when interviewed by the *Berkshire Eagle* in 1942. Undset had fled her home in Norway when Nazis invaded in 1940. Undset had long opposed Hitler, and her books were banned in Germany. She declined to discuss the war, telling a reporter, "I don't like arm-chair strategists."

Undset didn't have much to say about her writing, either: "I am always working," she said from her temporary home, artist Robert P. Ensign's Brookbend Tavern in Monterey.

Born in Denmark, the writer absorbed an early fascination with old cultures from her father, archaeologist Ingvald Undset. He is depicted as the father in the cycle *Kristin Lavransdatter* (1920–22).

The Undset home was filled with books, and Sigrid gravitated to old Norse sagas. The family fell into poverty upon the father's death. Sigrid attended the school of Ragna Nielsen and received a secretarial certificate from Christiania Commercial College in 1898. She worked as a secretary for German Electric in Oslo, gradually selling more and more of her fiction until she was sufficiently successful to quit the day job. A marriage to Anders C. Svarsvad in 1911 yielded three children but ended in annulment in 1924, when she embraced the Roman Catholic faith. She became the foremost Catholic author in Scandinavia.

The best known of her thirty-six books, *Kristin Lavransdatter* is the story of a young woman who defies her father to wed a man she loves. The marriage is not without consequence: it alienates Kristin's father and results in the suicide of her husband's former mistress and mother of his two children out of wedlock. (Norwegian actress Liv Ullmann played Kristin in a 1995 film version.) The story brings fifteenth-century Norway vividly alive.

SIGRID UNDSET
1882 – 1949 **NORGE 2.00**
1982

Prize-winning novelist Sigrid Undset was a refugee from Norway
during World War II who settled in Monterey. *Norway postage
stamp, 1982.*

"She is a great story-teller, with a profound and realistic knowledge of the
labyrinths of the human mind—at all times and in all places," according to
biographer Gidske Anderson.

Undset was as terse in accepting international honor as she was fielding
the local reporter's queries. Her acceptance speech for the Nobel Prize for
Literature consisted of eleven sentences praising Sweden.

After the war, Undset returned to Lillehammer. But of her summer home,
she said she would "remember [the Berkshire hills] as one of the most
beautiful spots in the world."

Undset's image appeared on a 2-kroner Norway commemorative postage
stamp in 1982.

Next door to Monterey Library, the old inn is now Brookbend Condominiums.

COZZENS AND LEWIS IN WILLIAMSTOWN, MAILER IN STOCKBRIDGE

Among works by James Gould Cozzens (1903–1978) is *Guard of Honor* (1948), a Pulitzer Prize–winning war novel. He and his wife, literary agent Sylvia Bernice Baumgarten Cozzens, acquired Shadow Brook Farm, the J. Ritchie Kimball estate on Oblong Road in Williamstown, in 1958. Cozzens abandoned his place in New Jersey because new electric power lines destroyed his vista. Here he could enjoy Mount Greylock unimpeded.

The writer sought seclusion and seldom spoke with townspeople on his trips to the post office. Cozzens preferred to observe rather than mingle. "What I want to do is present stuff in the form of true experience," Cozzens wrote in his notebook on November 12, 1967, "the happenings of living life as I have found them to happen."

The Cozzenses left in 1971 for Florida's warmer climate.

The first American to win the Nobel Prize for Literature, Sinclair Lewis (1885–1951) was more outgoing. He won (and refused) the Pulitzer Prize for *Arrowsmith* in 1926. Two decades later, Minnesota-born Lewis leased a house at Thorvale Farm on Oblong Road in Williamstown. He wrote *Kingsblood Royal* and *The God-Seeker* here. He called "the valley from the Hoosic River north to Bennington the most beautiful scenery in the world."

The Lewises left in 1948 for a new home in Rome.

Norman Mailer (1923–2007) won the Pulitzer Prize for his first novel, *The Naked and the Dead* (1948). Already maintaining residences in New York and Maine, Mailer acquired the seventy-year-old, fifteen-room brown-shingled

Sinclair Lewis loved rural Williamstown's panoramas in the 1960s. *Library of Congress.*

mansion Wyndcote on Yale Hill in Stockbridge in 1972 when his book *Saint George and the Godfather* appeared in print.

The writer negotiated a million-dollar contract while living here—and he made frequent trips to the Rexall pharmacy in Great Barrington, owner Bernard Green told me, for heavy conversations with his divorce lawyer from a telephone booth in the rear of the store.

Mailer sold the Stockbridge home in 1977 to James Buckley, founder of the newspaper *Screw*. Mailer went back to New York to run for mayor.

Norman Mailer had a Stockbridge retreat in the 1970s. *Library of Congress.*

VI
REAL FOLKS

NOT THE LAST OF THE MOHICANS

Figures from Berkshire County's eighteenth-century history have appeared in fiction.

Colonel Ephraim Williams Jr. of Stockbridge and Williamstown died in the Bloody Morning Scout near Lake George in September 1755. He left funds to establish Williams College. A novel about the New England frontier, *Salute to Courage* (1967) by William Tyler Arms (1904–1970), finds protagonist David Bradbury, a newly recruited ranger, becoming enthralled with the young half-Indian girl Ulalia. These are times of turmoil. Williams appears—and dies offstage. British general Jeffery Amherst, who marched soldiers across South Berkshire in late autumn 1758, appears, on his way to attack Fort Carillon. The dialogue of Indian characters is overly Tonto-ish. But the writer has a good handle on the past. Arms, who attended Williams College, reported for the *Christian Science Monitor* and *New York Times*.

Boys of the Border (1907), the third entry in the Old Deerfield series by Mary Prudence Wells Smith (1840–1930), visits the same conflict of 1746–55. At Fort Massachusetts in North Adams, we meet "Captain Ephraim Williams, who was commander of the whole line of forts along the northwest border."

Two-time Newbury Award winner Elizabeth George Speare (1908–1994) set *The Prospering* (1967) in early Stockbridge, then called Indian Town, and relates the story of missionary John Sergeant and his conversion of Indians to Christianity. The main character is Elizabeth, the youngest of three daughters of Ephraim Williams Sr. "In the difficult years of her growing up, Elizabeth witnesses the evolution of the mission settlement into the gracious and beautiful town of Stockbridge," a jacket blurb says.

Alice Mary (Ross) Colver (1892–1988) wrote *The Measure of the Years* (1954) about the struggles of Prue Martin's pioneer family in the mission community Indian Town. A summer resident, Colver researched the book at the Historical Room at the Stockbridge Library. According to a book jacket blurb, Colver "began to write when she was in her teens. Actually, she completed her first book shortly after being graduated from Wellesley College, and it was promptly accepted and published. It was a story for girls, and she has continued to be interested in young people, and to write for them, while pursuing her career as a novelist." Colver wrote the Joan Foster series and *Vicky Barnes, Junior Hospital Volunteer* (1966).

Still in Indian Town in the 1750s, Solomon, the Mohican hero of *With Sacred Honor* (2012) by William T. Johnson, is in love with an English woman, Catherine, with the complexities that entails. He becomes a scout with Hobbs's company of rangers to fight the French and Iroquois.

And Kenneth Roberts (1885–1957) in *Northwest Passage* (1937) features the historical character Captain Robert Rogers and his famed rangers—which historically included a company of Mohicans from Stockbridge under the command of Captain Jacob. One Stockbridge ranger really did die during the raid on the Abenaki town of St. Francis in Quebec in 1756, and three were captured. Another novel by Maine-born Roberts, *Rabble in Arms* (1933), is about the second invasion of Canada during the American Revolution and includes fictional versions of real-life Patriots John Brown and James Easton of Pittsfield and John Fellows of Sheffield.

Berkshire Historical Figures in Literature

To continue our survey, ladies first. We'll start with a woman who fought for her freedom in a courtroom.

Bett, a domestic in the John Ashley household in Sheffield, won her release from slavery in a trial held in Great Barrington in 1781. She became Elizabeth Freeman, or Mumbet to the children in the Theodore Sedgwick household she nannied in Stockbridge. Her story is told in the young readers book *Mumbet: The Story of Elizabeth Freeman* (1970) by Harold W. Felton and the young adult book *A Free Woman on God's Earth* (2009) by Jana Laiz and Ann-Elizabeth Barnes.

In *New-England Tale* (1822), Catharine Sedgwick blended Mumbet and "Crazy Sue" Dunham, an eccentric white woman who roamed the county, to shape the character Crazy Bet:

> *Poor Bet was sure to follow in every funeral procession, and sometimes she would thrust herself amidst the mourners, and say, "the dead could not rest in their graves, if they were not followed there by one true mourner." She has been seen to spring forward when the men were carelessly placing the coffin in the grave with the head to the east, and exclaim, "are ye heathens, that ye serve the dead thus? Know ye not the 'Lord cometh in the east.'" She always lingered behind after the crowd had dispersed, and busily moved and removed the sods; and many a time has she fallen asleep, with her head resting on the new-made grave, for, she said, there was no sleep so quiet as "where the wicked did not trouble."*

Great Barrington native Laura Ingersoll Secord became a Canadian heroine just before the Battle of Beaverdams in Upper Canada (Ontario) during the War of 1812. She is depicted in the children's book *Laura: A Childhood Tale of Laura Secord* (2000) by Maxine Trottier. She's also in the young adult novel *Laura's Choice* (1993) by Connie Brummel Crook (b. 1930). And Crook wrote a picture book, *Laura Secord's Brave Walk* (2000), for a younger audience. Laura is the only individual from Berkshire history to appear in a comic book. Two, in fact. She has an eight-page story in American Graphics No. 2, *Victory at Niagara and Laura Secord, Heroine of the War of 1812* (1957). And there's a six-page story, "Laura Secord: The Brave Messenger," in *Treasure Chest of Fun & Fact* (1967). She shows up in a folk song, too, "Secord's Warning," by Joe Grant and Steve Ritchie, recorded on the Ontario group Tanglefoot's 2003 CD *Captured Alive*.

Rachel Field's *All This and Heaven Too* (1938) fictionalized the life of a young nineteenth-century French governess, Henriette Delvzy-Desportes, who sought refuge in America after the Duc de Praslin, her employer, was jailed for murdering his wife—some said because the duke was romantically involved with the governess. Desportes married the author's great-uncle, the Reverend Henry Martyn Field, and they lived on Prospect Hill in Stockbridge. The book depicts the excitement of Henry's brother Cyrus W. Field laying the Atlantic cable, and Bryant, Stowe and Kemble appear.

Edith Wharton is the subject of *The Age of Desire* (2012) by Jennie Fields (b. 1953). The story is related through the points of view of Wharton and her governess, Anna Bahlmann.

Carol De Chellis Hill (b. 1942) included Wharton in her literary mystery *Henry James' Midnight Song* (1994).

Someone sends Adams-born suffrage leader Susan B. Anthony a threatening letter in 1891, and Millicent Davies and her partner, Art MacDuff, formerly with Pinkerton, set about to find out who in William Freeman's mystery *The Plot to Kill Susan B. Anthony* (2011).

To look at the gents, we'll start at the American Revolution.

His ride to alert Patriots of the pending skirmish with British soldiers in Concord and Lexington in 1775 has not been verified to the satisfaction of all historians, but Israel Bissell (who later settled in Hinsdale) nevertheless appears in a children's book by Marjorie N. Allen (b. 1931) of Pittsfield and Alice Schick (b. 1946) of Monterey: *The Remarkable Ride of Israel Bissell as Related by Molly the Crow* (1976). A New Hampshire native, Allen wrote several works for children. Schick wrote children's books with her husband, Joel.

There's no doubting the veracity of Colonel Henry Knox's 1776 winter transport of cannon from Fort Ticonderoga to Cambridge to assist General George Washington. Martin R. Ganzglass, an attorney in Washington, D.C., and once a Peace Corps volunteer in Somalia, wrote *Cannons for the Cause* (2014) from the perspective of sixteen-year-old teamster Willem Stoner's experiences helping Knox. The Knox Trail crosses Berkshire from Alford and Egremont east to Otis and Blandford.

Knox is also a character in John Jakes's Kent Family Chronicles. In *The Rebels* (1975), Philip Kent treks through the snow with Knox. Jakes (b. 1932) specializes in sprawling family saga series.

Thomas "The Fighting Parson" Allen and a contingent of Pittsfield Minutemen fought the British at Bennington (actually, Walloomsac, New York) in August 1777. Wallace Bruce (1844–1914), Freemason, Chautauquan and professional commemorator, wrote a twelve-stanza verse titled "Parson Allen's Ride" for the 1877 centennial in Bennington. It was widely reprinted in newspapers and anthologies.

At war's end, there was economic turmoil throughout New England. Edward Bellamy (1850–1898), on commission by Clark W. Bryan, publisher of the *Berkshire Courier* in Great Barrington, wrote a romance of Shays' Rebellion, *The Duke of Stockbridge*. The sympathetic telling was serialized in the weekly newspaper from January 1 to July 2, 1879, but wasn't issued as a book until 1900, in a version revised by a cousin, Francis

Bellamy. Harvard University Press brought out an unexpurgated edition in 1962. The book fictionalizes real incidents of Shays' Rebellion—the last skirmish of which took place in Sheffield in 1778—and has scenes in West Stockbridge (at Elijah Williams's ironworks), Stockbridge (Mumbet protects the Sedgwick silver) and Great Barrington. Characters such as "Duke" Perez Hamlin, Dr. Oliver Partridge and Parson Stephen West are based on historical figures. Bellamy was born and lived most of his life in Chicopee Falls. In 1868, he toured Germany, where the sight of city slums sparked an interest in the economically dispossessed. In 1880, Bellamy and his brother C.J. founded the *Springfield Penny* (later *Daily*) *News*. Edward is best known for the utopian book *Looking Backward* (1888), which sold several million copies.

Michael Thorn (b. 1951), who grew up in Wembley and Sussex, England, wrote *Pen Friends* (1988) to explore the relationship between Melville and Hawthorne. "Troubled by the symptoms of artistic guilt and an unsatisfactory home life,

Melville is philosophically hungry for a calmness of mind which he believes Hawthorne to possess, and energetically pursues the older man," a dust jacket blurb notes.

Two other writers from the 1850 Monument Mountain ascent—Holmes and James T. Fields—along with Longfellow and Lowell are amateur detectives in the historical thriller *The Dante Club* (2003) by Matthew Pearl (b. 1975). The bookish quartet solves a series of grisly killings in Boston.

National Book Award nominee Karen Shepard of Williamstown wrote *The Celestials* (2013), a novel about seventy-five Chinese factory workers hired as strikebreakers at the Calvin Sampson shoe factory in North Adams in 1870. When Sampson's wife, Julia, gives birth to a mixed-race child, the novel raises issues of identity, alienation

Karen Shepard turned a North Adams incident into a historical novel, *The Celestials*. *Barry Goldstein.*

and exile. The author is a Chinese American woman who grew up in New York City. She teaches writing and literature at Williams College.

Judith Eichler Weber (b. 1938), who owned a condominium in Williamstown, wrote about the same incident, changing the historical names slightly in *Forbidden Friendship* (1991). Molly, whose father, Thomas Simpson, owns the shoe factory, becomes fond of Chen Li, one of the Chinese workers she is tutoring.

A third of Winthrop Knowlton's 1983 novel *False Premises* takes place in "Ellsworth Falls," a fictionalized Great Barrington. Clarence Starcliffe, the protagonist's spindly grandfather and inventor, lighted the town's main street with alternating-current electricity in March 1886—just as Knowlton's real-life grandfather, William Stanley, did in Great Barrington. "All that March day a gusting wind blew lumps of wet snow against the store windows on Main Street," writes Knowlton (b. 1930). "It shook the looping strands of rubber-insulated wire Clarence Starcliffe had strung through the elm trees. It made the early arrival shiver on the hard wooden seats of their buckboards. Women and children sought shelter in the Ellsworth Inn; the men went off in another direction, into the saloons along Railroad Street."

VII

GENRE FICTION

Mystery Writers Who Have Been Here

Mystery authors and their fictional detectives were drawn to western Massachusetts. First we'll look at writers who have been in the Berkshires and then at sleuths who have been here.

The world's best-known literary crime fighter has a Berkshire tie.

Dozens of writers have picked up Arthur Conan Doyle's mantle to continue the casework of master investigator Sherlock Holmes. The pipe-smoking detective's client is Queen Victoria in Otis resident Edward B. Hanna's pastiche, *The Whitechapel Horrors* (1992), for example. And Tracy Mack and Michael Citrin of Great Barrington write young adult mysteries featuring the Baker Street Irregulars. Mack said she always wanted to be Harriet the Spy. Citron said he grew up reading Conan Doyle.

Another well-known fictional crime solver, Honolulu policeman Charlie Chan, was the creation of Earl Derr Biggers (1884–1933), a newspaper columnist whose first play, *If You're Only Human*, was staged at the Colonial Theatre in Pittsfield in 1912. His novel *The Seven Keys to Baldpate* (1913) used the Aspinwall Hotel in Lenox (where he resided) as the model for an inn where the protagonist takes a room in order to complete a manuscript.

Largely forgotten are the Dennis Tyler mystery novels written under the pen name "Diplomat" from 1930 to 1935 by John Franklin Carter (1897–1967). Carter's hero was a career diplomat and amateur sleuth, mirroring to a degree his creator's vocation as a political journalist. Carter grew up in Williamstown, where his father was rector of St. John's Church. Carter in the 1920s was a private secretary to the American ambassador at Rome. He wrote for the *London Daily Chronicle* and the *New York Times* before serving as an economic specialist in the State Department. "A serious infection in childhood left Carter 'with bad eyes and a leaky heart,' and he learned to write 'in self-defense against a world which is, among children at least, thoroughly contemptuous of weaklings,'" according to Stanley J. Kunitz and Howard Haycraft.

J. Allan Dunn (1872–1941), London-born journalist, Explorers Club member and author of more than one thousand stories and forty novels of

J. Allan Dunn was by his wife's side during her sensational murder trial in 1919. Boston Post.

private eyes, pirates and cowboys, house-hopped in Lanesboro, Lenox and Pittsfield in 1917–20. He sold stories to *Adventure, Outdoor Stories, Gang World, Dime Detective, Wild West Weekly, Short Stories, Sunset* and *Boy's Life*. His thirty-one stories of police detective Gordon Manning's pursuit of The Griffin, king of the extortionists, for *Detective Fiction Weekly* were collected in three reprint volumes in 2014–15. He dedicated his 1921 novel *The Man Trap* to "My friend, Frank M. White (deputy sheriff), Pittsfield, Massachusetts." Tragically, his wife, mentally distressed Gladys Courvoisier Dunn, spent a year in the Berkshire County House of Correction after confessing to manslaughter in the death of their two-year-old son, Joseph Allan Dunn Jr., in 1918—a victim of her own attempt at suicide.

Also English-born, Hugh C. Wheeler (1912–1987) served in the U.S. Army Medical Corps during World War II and became a naturalized American citizen. Collaborating with another Englishman, R. Wilson "Rickie" Webb (1901–1966), he was the pseudonymous "Patrick Quentin," "Q. Patrick" and "Jonathan Stagge."

Webb and Wheeler closeted themselves at Hickory Farm in Tyringham in 1939 to write mysteries. Webb devised a plot, Wheeler fleshed it out and then they honed a final draft as Wheeler typed. The writers in 1944 purchased Twin Hills Farm in Monterey. Richard V. Happel wrote, "Although [Wheeler] frequently visited New York City, he said, 'I find I can't write there at all. In fact, Monterey is the only place where I can really write.'"

Webb moved to France in 1952. Wheeler on his own continued Quentin mysteries featuring Broadway producer Peter Duluth and his actress wife, Iris Murdoch. He is best remembered, however, for his screenplays and dialogue for the musicals *A Little Night Music* (1973), *Candide* (1973) and *Sweeney Todd* (1979). All three won Tony Awards.

"Elizabeth Daly was my aunt," Eleanor Boylan (1916–2007) told me, "and left me the copyright to her books. I've been a writer of short mystery fiction for years, and my agent finally persuaded me to try a full-length novel and 'bring back [Henry] Gamadge.' Actually, I've brought back Clara. Henry has recently died." The closest Daly (1878–1967) came to using a Berkshire setting was in *Evidence of Things Seen* (1943), in which Henry and Clara vacation in the Connecticut Berkshires. Boylan, however, spent childhood summers in the Great Barrington–Egremont–Sheffield area. Boylan continued the Gamadge series beginning with *Working Murder* (1989). In *Murder Observed* (1990), the locale bounces between New York City and Lake Winifred, which is "in the southern Berkshires, halfway between ritzy Sharon, Connecticut, and rural Sheffield, Massachusetts."

Milton Bass (1923–2014) of Richmond, longtime entertainment editor for the *Berkshire Eagle*, wrote books featuring Benny Freedman, a half-Jewish, half-Irish homicide detective. In *The Moving Finger* (1986), the hero confronts a crazed California cult leader. *The Belfast Connection* (1989) takes Freedman to Northern Ireland, seeking the family of his Irish mother. He becomes involved in a murder and IRA terrorism. Later mysteries *The Half-Hearted Detective* (1992) and *The Broken-Hearted Detective* (1994) feature Vinnie Altobelli, a police officer forced to retire after suffering a heart attack.

Carolyn G. Heilbrun (1926–2003) was a college professor by vocation and a mystery writer by avocation. "She first became Amanda Cross in 1963 when her children were young and in camp," according to *Wellesley* magazine. "It was peaceful in the country, and, having long read detective stories, but feeling dissatisfied by many of them, she decided to try 'dashing one off herself.'" Her 1967 Kate Fansler mystery *The James Joyce Murder* (1967) takes place in an ill-disguised version of the town of Alford, where she had a summer home. Her life ended in suicide.

A Pennsylvania native, Richard Lipez (b. 1938) of Becket worked at the Peace Corps' national headquarters in Washington, D.C., after serving three years in Ethiopia. Using the pen name "Richard Stevenson," he has written mysteries featuring a gay Albany private investigator, Donald Strachey, and his partner, Timmy Callahan, a legislative aide to a New York senator. In *Tongue Tied* (2003), Strachey, searching for a kidnap victim, makes a side trip to the Berkshire Woolly Llama Cheese farm (fake), just down the road from Monterey Chevre goat cheese Farm (real) in Monterey. In *Death Vows* (2008), Strachey takes on a gay Great Barrington couple as clients and investigates the background of a man about to marry a friend of theirs—not realizing the tangle he is about to get into involving Mafia thugs and homophobic relatives.

Lipez counters the usual gay stereotypes in mystery fiction; his villains are neither psychopaths nor misfits. Four of his books were filmed by HereTV, a gay-oriented cable channel.

"The Strachey books haven't changed a lot since the first one, *Death Trick*, came out in 1981," Lipez told me. "Strachey and Timmy, amazingly, have hardly aged at all, a feat I have not managed for myself. But gay life in America has changed over the years—from the golden age of gay lib to the horrors of the AIDS crisis to the gay-marriage struggles—and the books do reflect those changes. The next one, the fourteenth, *Why Stop at Vengeance?*, is about American religious fundamentalists who have failed to stop gay progress in the U.S. and have now taken their unholy crusade overseas to Africa and Eastern Europe."

Daniel M. Klein (b. 1939) of Great Barrington mixed mystery and rock-and-roll for four mystery novels featuring Elvis Presley, beginning with *Kill Me Tender* (2000). Klein immersed himself in Elvis lore. The hardest part, he said in a conversation, was getting the singer's vocal cadence right. Klein's earlier novel *Embryo* (1981) is about the price paid by women who consult a pregnancy expert. His suspense novels are *Wavelength* (1982) and *Beauty Sleep* (1990). *Magic Time* (1984) follows the fortunes of five friends, Harvard graduates, who took part in Timothy Leary's first LSD experiment in 1961. His novel *The History of Now* (2009) recasts the history of Great Barrington's Main Street and the loves and agonies of a movie theater projectionist.

Born in Delaware, Klein graduated from Harvard with a degree in philosophy. After spending a year in Europe, he became a caseworker in the New

Top: Richard Lipez as "Richard Stevenson" writes mystery novels featuring a gay private eye, Don Strachey. *Richard Lipez.*

Left: Daniel M. Klein has written four novels featuring Elvis Presley as a crime solver. *Bernard A. Drew, 1981.*

York City welfare department. In the 1960s, he wrote for television's *Candid Camera* and *Reach for the Stars*.

Parnell Hall (b. 1944), once a Lenox resident, has written mysteries featuring Stanley Hastings. In *Juror* (1991), Hastings is called for trial duty—and when one of his fellow jurors is found strangled, Hastings is the prime suspect. The author has a second series, about the Puzzle Lady, and a third, under the "J.P. Hailey" byline, featuring lawyer Steve Winslow. In *The Naked Typist* (1990), Winslow must solve the "Red-Headed League"–like puzzle of why Kelly Blaine was hired to transcribe an elderly tycoon's memoirs—while sitting nude in an office.

Wayne Barcomb (b. 1933), who grew up in North Adams, took up writing after a two-decade career with a Boston textbook publishing house. He and his wife relocated from Cohasset, Massachusetts, to Sarasota, Florida, in 1991, and there he wrote four books, including two featuring a private eye, Sam Wallace, for a small press. St. Martin's brought out his first thriller featuring NYPD homicide detective Frank Russo in 2009. *The Hunted* includes scenes in North Adams.

Andrew Bergman (b. 1946), a screenwriter and director with a home in Sheffield, wrote two mystery novels featuring Jack LeVine, *The Big Kiss-Off of 1944* (1974) and *Hollywood and LeVine* (1975).

Archer Mayor (b. 1950) of Vermont writes the Joe Gunther series set mostly in the Green Mountain State, with occasional travels elsewhere. Mayor, when a student at Yale, worked one summer for the *Berkshire Eagle* in Pittsfield, he told me. *The Ragman's Memory* (1996) brings the hero to North Adams in search of clues.

Charles O'Brien of Williamstown, retired from Western Illinois University, has written ten historical mystery novels featuring Anne Cartier (former music hall entertainer and now tutor to deaf children) and her husband, Paul de Saint-Martin (commander of the Gendarmerie Nationale). The books are set in England and France before the French Revolution. In *Death of a Robber Baron* (2013), O'Brien's first Gilded Age Mystery, private-investigator-in-training Pamela Thompson investigates mismanagement—and murder—at palatial "Broadmore Hall" in the Berkshires in 1893.

Elise Title worked for six years as a psychotherapist in the Massachusetts correctional system. A Lee resident, her suspense novels include *Romeo* (1998), about a man who preys on successful women.

A North Adams native and former *Advocate* newspaper reporter, Beth Saulnier features Gen-X journalist Alex Bernier in five crime novels, including *Reliable Sources* (1999) and *Ecstasy* (2009). The setting is a mash of her hometown and Ithaca, New York.

The first cozy mystery by Mary Moody of Great Barrington, *A Killing in Antiques* (2011), features dealer Lucy St. Elmo. The story takes place at the Brimfield outdoor antiques market.

A part-time resident, Jim Weikert (b. 1941) set the first of his tax accountant–sleuth Jay Jasen series, *Casualty Loss* (1991), partially at a vacation home in Otis.

Leslie Wheeler (b. 1945) said she splits her time between Cambridge and New Marlborough. She launched her Miranda Lewis mystery series with *Murder at Plimoth Plantation* in 2001 and has continued with other books set at living history venues.

Another second-homer, Liza Gyllenhaal disguises West Stockbridge as the setting of her fourth novel, *Bleeding Heart* (2014), a "gardening thriller."

MYSTERY WRITERS WHOSE CHARACTERS HAVE BEEN HERE

Some crime novelists used Berkshire settings.

Bernard A. DeVoto (1897–1955), occupant of *Harper's* "The Easy Chair" beginning in 1935 and an editor of the *Saturday Review of Literature* starting the next year, wrote mysteries under the "John August" pseudonym. His 1943 novel *Advance Agent*, serialized in *Collier's*, is set "in the town of Windham, Berkshire County, Massachusetts." The villain is a Lenox millionaire and German sympathizer who covers his sabotage plot by giving pro-peace speeches.

Ben Benson (1915–1959), recovering from wounds suffered at the Battle of the Bulge, began to write police procedurals featuring Massachusetts State Police. "The Big Kiss-off" in *Ellery Queen's Mystery Magazine* for February 1956 takes place on Route 2 near North Adams. A clever trooper gets the best of a female fugitive.

Dennis Lynds (1924–2005) used the pen name "Michael Collins" for the Dan Fortune crime novel *The Silent Scream* (1975), which takes place in part in Great Barrington.

Award-winning novelist Ira Levin (1929–2007), best known as author of *Rosemary's Baby* (1967), included references to Lenox and Pittsfield in his thriller about Nazi hunter Yakov Liebermann, *The Boys from Brazil* (1976).

Donald E. Westlake (1933–2008) had a home in Ancramdale, New York, so knew the Great Barrington of which he wrote. A prolific writer of mystery and crime fiction under his own name and as "Richard Stark," "Samuel Holt" and "Tucker Coe," he alternated serious and humorous stories. Typically, Sara Joslyn stumbles across a body on her first day as a reporter for a sleazy tabloid in *Trust Me on This* (1988). The heroine's mother lives in Great Barrington. Another character motors through Great Barrington in *The Ax* (1997). In the Richard Stark novel *Firebreak* (2002), career thief Parker abandons a stolen Volvo in Great Barrington. And the career loser–thief Dortmunder mentions Great Barrington in *What's So Funny?* (2007).

Manhattanite Lawrence Block (b. 1938) has written about the burglaries of Bernie Rhodenbarr; the capers of Evan Tanner, the spy who couldn't sleep; and the victims of Keller, the stamp-collecting hired killer. His Matthew Scudder books about a former cop and recovering alcoholic include *A Dance at the Slaughterhouse* (1991), in which the hero and his girlfriend vacation in the Berkshires.

J.A. Jance (b. 1944) sets most of her Sheriff Joanna Brady mysteries in Arizona, but for the *Remains of Innocence* (2013), she starts the story in Great Barrington, where Liza Machett is cleaning out her hoarder-mother's home. She finds a fortune in cash hidden inside old magazines. "Great Barrington just caught my creative eye for some reason at the time I was starting the book. Happy accident," the author of fifty novels told me. Jance's is not quite the Great Barrington we know; the town doesn't have a truck stop diner, much less one that serves gravy and biscuits. And a cell tower in Stockbridge? Don't they wish.

Researchers for James Patterson (b. 1947) let him down

J.A. Jance's 2013 Arizona police procedural *Remains of Innocence* begins with a suspicious fire in Great Barrington. *Jerry Bauer.*

in the novel *Cross* (2006), in which FBI-agent-turned-psychologist Alex Cross pursues the man he believes killed his wife. The Butcher is staying in the town of Florida. Cross races to the house, but the Butcher isn't there. So Cross "drove to the town center and had lunch at a Denny's." Now, if you know Florida (population 752), you know it has no chain restaurant. The killer, meanwhile, has completed a hit on a woman in Stockbridge and is returning to Florida by way of the Massachusetts Turnpike. Really? The Pike will take you east to Boston or west to Albany, but it will *not* take you northeast to Florida. How Cross and the Butcher ever meet up…well, that's creative writing.

Cornelia Read of New Hampshire, in her second Madeline Dare series novel, *The Crazy School* (2010), brings the ex–California rich girl to the Berkshires to teach at the Santangelo Academy, a boarding school for troubled teens with dark secrets in Stockbridge (sounds suspiciously like the former DeSisto School). The time is 1989, the setting is "Wifflehead Mountain: a single peak tucked into the lush hills and canyons just west of Stockbridge."

Writing in the cozy style, Clea Simon's heroine Pru Marlowe is an animal psychic who has abandoned the big city to return to the Berkshires. Her sidekick is Wallis the cat. A recent title by the Somerville, Massachusetts author is *Panthers Play for Keeps* (2014), in which an apparent killer mountain lion is at large.

TANGLEWOOD'S CRIMINOUS TUNES

The world's second-best-known fictional crime fighter, Nancy Drew, solved a crime at Tanglewood, summer home to the Berkshire Symphony Orchestra.

The girl PI has appeared in nearly 500 books since 1930. Author "Carolyn Keene" is a pen name made up by Edward L. Stratemeyer (1862–1930), an industrious fiction syndicator. Stratemeyer came up with characters for juvenile hardcover book series and farmed them out to publishers. He hired ghostwriters to flesh out his storylines. The formulaic books relied heavily on action and proved enduringly popular. In *Love Notes* (1995), the 109th entry in the Nancy Drew Files, the heroine is in "Westbridge," which is "nestled in the Berkshire Mountains," to attend a well-known piano competition, the "Muscatonic Summer Music Festival"—Tanglewood in disguise. Someone is making mysterious threats against a pianist.

There have been other ill doings at the summer music fest.

Right: Lucille Kallen, a television comedy writer, set one of her murder mysteries at Tanglewood. *Bernard A. Drew, 1980.*

Below: Gerald Elias details the inner workings of the Boston Symphony Orchestra in his mystery series. *Nicholas Steffens.*

Lucille Kallen (1926–1999), who scripted television's *Your Show of Shows* from 1949 to 1954, brought her amateur detectives here in *The Tanglewood Murder* (1980). Weekly newspaper publisher C.B. Greenfield and his chief reporter, Maggie Rome, fall upon mischief and mayhem among BSO (Boston Symphony Orchestra) members. Kallen explained that she wrote the book during a stay at Wheatleigh in Stockbridge. "The natural beauty here really symbolizes everything that is worthwhile in life, and violence represents what's awful. Tanglewood threatened by violence represents the world and things of value being attacked by 'forces,'" she said.

Gerald Elias (b. 1953), who splits his time between Salt Lake City and West Stockbridge, has been a violinist with the Boston Symphony Orchestra and the Utah Symphony. Today, besides filling in with the BSO at Tanglewood in summers, he composes music and writes mysteries—such as *Death and Transfiguration* (2012), his fourth book featuring the blind violinist Daniel Jacobus. Jacobus (no surprise) has a home in West Stockbridge. The author uses Tanglewood as backdrop for his insider's perspective on classical musicians and offensive conductors. Of his writing career, the author told critic Andrew L. Pincus, "One needs to be passionate about anything one does, I think, to get the most profound results."

BOSTON PIs

Name a Boston-area writer or fictional detective in the 1980s and '90s—he probably visited the Berkshires.

Robert B. Parker (1932–2010) rejuvenated the private detective genre with his hero Spenser and sidekick Hawk. Spenser makes his way to the Berkshires in *Early Autumn* (1980), in which he is looking for a missing mother: "We started in Stockbridge, because Paul and I agreed that Stockbridge was where we'd buy a place if we were on the run…We left Pearl [the dog] in the car with the windows part open diagonally across from the Red Lion Inn, walked across the street to the biggest real estate office on the main street in Stockbridge, and showed the picture of Patty Giacomin to a thick woman in a pair of green slacks and a pink turtleneck." In *Pastime* (1991), the private investigator is looking for another missing woman. "The Lenox cops may be the ultimate police machine for all I know. But small-town police forces often aren't, and I'm afraid if they start looking for Richie and your mother that they'll spook them for sure," Spenser tells his client. In the same book, "The

Motel Thirty in Lee had no objection to Pearl. They also would have had no objection to the Creature from the Black Lagoon—or Madonna."

George V. Higgins (1939–1999) sets part of *The Mandeville Talent* (1991) in the imaginary town of "Shropshire," near Lenox and Pittsfield. A corporate attorney solves a decades-old mystery. The Brockton-born writer was a former assistant U.S. district attorney. His first novel, *The Friends of Eddie Coyle*, was a finalist for the National Book Award in fiction in 1972.

Edgar Award–winning Rick Boyer (b. 1943) wrote nine mystery novels about dentist-sleuth Charlie Adams and two about Sherlock Holmes. In *Gone to Earth* (1990), Doc Adams is fixing up a farm he and his wife have purchased in "Humphrey" (somewhere near Otis) when they discover four Harley-Davidson motorcycles hidden in a barn—and six skeletons in graves nearby. "I spent over two hours scanning the hills, fields and woods, including the towns of Great Barrington and Stockbridge," Adams tells us. "If there is a prettier town on earth than Stockbridge, Mass., I haven't seen it."

Jeremiah Healy (1948–2014) introduced his series detective John Francis Cuddy to the Lee and Stockbridge area in *Blunt Darts* (1985). A character in the story is said to have been a patient at a sanitarium in "the Berkshires near Tanglewood."

In the 1985 mystery *Follow the Sharks* by William G. Tapply (1940–2009), Red Sox star player Eddie Donagan's son has been kidnapped and he hires lawyer-detective Brady Coyne to find him. Coyne's investigation drives him across the commonwealth to a farm in Lanesboro. *The Seventh Enemy* (1995) includes action in the vicinity of Florida and Charlemont on the Deerfield River.

Dennis Lehane (b. 1965) grew up in Dorchester, Massachusetts. The author of *Mystic River* (2001) and *Shutter Island* (2003) brought a team of thugs to Pittsfield in the Edgar Award–winning, Prohibition-era novel about a Boston police captain's son gone bad, *Live by Night* (2012). Joe Coughlin and the Bartolo brothers knock down the First National Bank, kill three city police officers and trigger a commonwealth-wide dragnet.

The Devious Mind of Judson Philips

Judson Philips (1903–1989) frequently described South Berkshire and northwest Connecticut settings in his books. And why not? That's where he lived.

"I started writing mysteries as Judson Philips," he told me in 1978.

> *But Dodd, Mead & Co. was offering a Red Badge Mystery Prize, and in 1938 they had no one they wanted to give it to. The author had to be unpublished. I had just finished a book without a running character, and they said they would give me the prize and publish the book if I took a new name.*
>
> *My middle name is Pentecost, and Hugh Pentecost was an uncle of mine who was a prominent lawyer in New York in the 1890s. I've never been able to get away from that name. To this day, I get more for a Pentecost book than for a Philips one.*

Most of the Pentecost tales feature the hotelier Pierre Chambrun.

Philips contributed forty thousand to fifty thousand words of fiction a month in the 1930s and '40s to pulp fiction magazines such as *Detective Fiction Weekly* (Park Avenue Hunt Club stories). He worked up to the *Saturday Evening Post* and *American Magazine*. At the time of our conversation, his main mystery short story market was *Ellery Queen's Mystery Magazine*.

Philips was born in Northfield, Massachusetts, the son of an opera singer and an actress. He was a sports reporter while in high school. He co-wrote movie scripts, including John Barrymore's first talkie, *General Crack*, and storyplays for *The Web*, *Studio One* and other television dramas. He adapted Father Brown stories for radio.

Philips moved to North Canaan after World War II. He was founder and producer at Sharon Playhouse from 1955 to 1970.

One of his Julian Quist stories, *Deadly Trap* (1978), involves action at "Lake Toromog" near Great Barrington. *The Judas Freak* (1974) setting is somewhere north of the same town.

His pseudonymous crime tales by "Hugh Pentecost" outsold ones published under his real name, Judson Philips. *Bernard A. Drew, 1979.*

"In the Uncle George stories," Philips said, "I wanted a small-town background, and it was easy to take Lakeville [called 'Lakeview' in the stories]. You wouldn't recognize it unless you lived around here. But it helps me in writing to use real places."

The plot of one 1958 short story anticipated the Chowchilla kidnapping in California in 1976—and prompted him to expand it into a novel, *The Day the Children Vanished* (1976). In the suspense tale, a mad man takes a school bus full of children—and vanishes. Philips said he let his imagination fly in thinking of old quarries and the section of Route 44 between East Canaan and Salisbury.

Philips in 1979 assumed yet another pen name, "Philip Owen," for *Mystery at a Country Inn*, published by Berkshire Traveller Press in Stockbridge. Philips did his research at the Red Lion Inn in Stockbridge and the White Hart in Salisbury.

He received the Mystery Writers of America Grand Master Award in 1973.

ELLIS PARKER BUTLER'S PHILO GUBB

After a year of high school, Iowan Ellis Parker Butler (1869–1937) became a clerk and salesman. He went to New York in 1897 to join the editorial staff of a trade paper. Later active in banking, he wrote funny stories and verses for *Woman's Home Companion, American Boy* and *Redbook*. He became president of the Authors League of America and the Players, Dutch Treat and Pomonock clubs. He died in the Williamsville section of West Stockbridge, where he and his wife, Ida, regularly rented a cottage on Water Street in summers beginning in 1928. He was speaker at the Laurel Hill Association's annual gathering in Stockbridge in August 1929.

Ellis Parker Butler's hero, Philo Gubb, took a correspondence course in criminology. *Bains News Service/Library of Congress.*

Butler's best-known story, *Pigs Is Pigs*, appeared in *American Magazine* in 1905. It recounts depot agent Mike Flannery's misadventures with a shipment of guinea pigs—a shipment that enlarges itself day by day as they go undelivered.

Butler's all-time most outrageous creation was *Philo Gubb, Correspondence School Detective* (1918). The book begins: "Walking close along the wall, to avoid the creaking floor boards, Philo Gubb, paper-hanger and student of the Rising Sun Detective Agency's Correspondence School of Detecting, tiptoed to the door of the bedroom he shared with the mysterious Mr. Critz."

Gubb's mail-order disguise kit came with multiple costumes, and he tries out each one, though children in town hail him on the street, easily seeing through his getup. Philo's first case, nabbing a con man, is solved by chance and after completing only eleven of the dozen lessons! His second case involves locating a millionaire's missing daughter. He finds her—she's now a fat lady in a circus—and falls in love. He accepts his reward in bogus mining stock, which leads to his third case.

THRILLER AND SUSPENSE WRITERS

Let's go undercover, into the world of espionage and suspense.

John P. Marquand (1893–1960) married Christina Davenport Sedgwick, one of the Stockbridge Sedgwicks, in 1922. He wrote while staying with her family in the Berkshires. He began his Mr. Moto espionage series in 1935, about the time the marriage unraveled. His best-known work is *The Late George Aply* (1937), a satire of Boston Brahmins that won the Pulitzer Prize. The Berkshire Theatre Festival staged the novel in 1946, with script by Marquand and George S. Kaufman.

F. Van Wyck Mason (1901–1978) attended Berkshire School in Sheffield (class of 1921), where he edited *Green & Grey* and was a member of the gun club. His later military experiences overseas provided material for historical novels and tales of intrigue featuring his series character, army intelligence officer Hugh North, who appeared in twenty-six books. Mason averaged two books a year beginning in 1928. *The Multi-million Dollar Murders* (1960), a North adventure, typically takes the hero on "the most perilous mission to which G-2 had ever assigned him."

Prentice Winchell (1895–1976), writing as "Stewart Sterling," in his novel-length spy thriller "The Eye of Death" in *G-Men Detective* for November 1941 describes a Nazi agent who is blackmailing a man into killing a well-known American scientist and inventor at his home in Great Barrington. There is skullduggery at a manufacturing plant in Great Barrington and at an establishment called Ye Olde Stone Jug Inn, which is modeled on Ye Olde Egremont Inn, part of Jug End Resort in South Egremont.

Dorothy Gilman (1923–2012), creator of the popular Mrs. Pollifax novels about a spinsterish geranium grower and sometimes CIA agent, was the daughter of a Pittsfield minister. She summered at the family's home on Pontoosuc Lake in Lanesboro. She married Edgar Butters, a teacher in New Jersey. Her stories *The Enchanted Caravan* and *Carnival Gypsy* had Pittsfield and Lanesboro settings. She researched her children's books at the Berkshire Athenaeum.

Don Pendleton (1927–1995) received a Naval Commendation Medal at Iwo Jima in 1945. He was an air traffic controller and later worked for General Electric and Lockheed. As a fiction writer, he introduced the action series hero Mack Bolan in *War Against the Mob* (1969). Bolan, alias The Executioner, returns from the Vietnam War to find his family has been killed by Mafia hit men. Born and raised in Pittsfield, of Welsh-Polish extraction, Bolan spends the first thirty-eight books in the series seeking revenge. Bolan's cover is assignment to the "ROTC unit at Franklin High, right here in Pittsfield." Pendleton in *Savage Fire* (1977) helps an old Pittsfield friend. Bolan went on to appear in more than six hundred paperback thrillers, after Pendleton's run, penned by hired writers.

Richard B. Sapir (1937–1987), a one-time Richmond Pond resident, with Warren B. Murphy in 1963 came up with a master of martial arts, Remo Williams, also called The Destroyer, a Vietnam War–era veteran now an agent of CURE. Williams's sidekick is Chiun, master of the martial art of Sinanju. The first adventure, *Created, The Destroyer*, came out in 1971. In a later book, *Assassins Play-Off* (1975), real-life Pittsfield astrologer Brian Kegan provides charts to Chiun.

Walter Wager (1924–2004) in *Telfon* (1975) describes the Soviet agent Dalchimski pursuing his quarry across the States. "Dalchimski liked the Berkshires," we read.

> *Those green valleys and mountains in Western Massachusetts were at least 10 degrees cooler than it had been in Dayton…He'd flown into Albany, moved on by bus to Pittsfield where he'd rented the car. The auto rental agency had helped him get the room down Route 7 in the smaller town of Stockbridge, explaining that the Red Lion Inn was booked solid for every*

weekend through Labor Day, but might be able to accommodate him for two days in the middle of the week.

Charles McCarry, born in Pittsfield in 1930, grew up in Plainfield. He was a reporter with *Stars & Stripes* and a roving editor with the *Saturday Evening Post* and *National Geographic*—the last covers as he served with the Central Intelligence Agency from 1958 to 1967. His experiences brought authenticity to his Paul Christopher espionage series that began with *The Miernik Dossier* (1973). *The Better Angels* (1979) includes a visit to a graveyard in West Stockbridge. The ending of McCarry's final Christopher tale, *Second Sight* (1991), takes place in Berkshire County.

Ethan Black is really Robert Reiss (b. 1951) of Becket, who writes hard-hitting thrillers featuring Conrad Voort, a New York police specialist in sex crimes. Reiss began the pseudonymous series with *The Broken Hearts Club* in 1999. The writer's German publisher issues the books under the byline Scott Canterbury.

PATRICIA HIGHSMITH WANTED TO SEE THE BODY

Crime novelist Patricia Highsmith (1921–1995) led a life nearly as troubled as that of her best-known fictional character Mr. Ripley, though her murders were always on paper, at least. She was an expatriate in Europe, where her misanthropy, fluctuating sexuality and brash plots were accepted, if not embraced. She was awarded the Grand Priz de Littérature Policière in 1957.

Her following in America was sporadic in her lifetime, despite a Crime Writers Association Silver Dagger Award in 1964 and her profound influence on other suspense writers. Recognition accelerated enormously in later decades, however, as her books returned to print and television, and theatrical films were made based on her works.

Born Mary Patricia Plantman, the author barely knew her father. Her parents broke up before she was born. Her relationship with her mother was strained. Patricia took the last name of her stepfather. She spent her childhood with her grandmother.

She graduated from Barnard College in New York in 1942, and after several inconsequential jobs, including one in retail and another providing plots to comic book script writers, she met Truman Capote, who arranged for her to go to the Yaddo arts colony in New York state. There she wrote a novel, *Strangers on a Train*. Its publication and the film by Alfred Hitchcock in 1951 brought her instant recognition.

The book set the tone for Highsmith's works that would appear over a forty-year period. They were criminous tales in which villains were sympathetic and innocent people sinned.

Her "novels and stories are, at their extreme, macabre expeditions into fear, more horror than crime, like Roald Dahl's *Tales of the Unexpected*. Even her less extreme works are bleak and unremitting, pushing the acceptable boundaries of suspense," Mike Ashley said.

In *Plotting and Writing Suspense Fiction*, she described a leisurely sojourn to Lenox in the early 1950s:

Patricia Highsmith mastered the moody thriller genre with books featuring Mr. Ripley. *Diogenes Verlag AG/courtesy Simone Sassen.*

> *I began* The Talented Mr. Ripley *in what I thought was a splendid mood, a perfect pace. I had taken a cottage in Massachusetts in the country near Lenox, and I spent the first three weeks there reading books from the excellent privately maintained library in Lenox, which, however, welcomes tourist patronage...*
>
> *My landlord, who lived not far away, was an undertaker, very voluble about his profession, though he drew the line at permitting me to visit his establishment and see the tree-shaped incision he made in the chest before stuffing the corpse. "What do you stuff the corpse with?" I asked. "Sawdust," he replied bluntly and matter-of-factly. I was toying with the idea of having Ripley engaged in a smuggling operation that involved a train ride from Trieste to Rome and Naples, during which Ripley would escort a corpse that was actually filled with opium. This was certainly a wrong tack, and I never wrote it that way, but this was why I was interested in seeing my landlord's corpses.*

The book features her best-realized, and only series, character, Tom Ripley. Ripley is a con artist who agrees to a millionaire's request and goes to Europe to locate the man's son, Dickie Greenleaf. Ripley is supposed to persuade Greenleaf to return home. Instead, he begins to fantasize he *is* Greenleaf. Ripley ends up killing the son and assuming his good life. Ripley is a fascinating character, though not particularly sympathetic.

WESTERN WRITERS

Berkshire has no cactus or sagebrush. Nevertheless, writers who lived here wrote about cowboys and outlaws, wagon trains, trail drives and Indians.

Frank Dorrance Hopley (1872–1933) was the son of an Otis minister and an avid collector of autographs. His collection included Thomas Edison, John J. Pershing, William Jennings Bryan and William H. Taft. He worked in New York City for thirty years as a secretary. He wrote magazine and newspaper stories and one novel. He turned out juvenile novels under house names for the Bob Chase and Jerry Ford series. After coming to Lee, he became "James Cody Ferris" to spin tales of the X-Bar-X Boys. A cover blurb describes these westerns: "The Manly boys know how to ride and shoot and take care of themselves under all circumstances, and the cowboys of the X-Bar-X Ranch are real cowboys—a bunch any reader would like to know."

Knowledgeable in the lore of Native Americans, one-time South Egremont, Sheffield and Great Barrington resident Chandler Whipple (1905–1977) was an editor at *Argosy*. His cowboy stories appeared in *Street & Smith's Western Story Magazine*, *Ranch Romances* and *Adventure*. His first book was *Under the Mesa Rim* (1940). Whipple later wrote the nonfiction book *The Indian and the White Man in New England* (1977).

Milton Bass, whose bio is found in the Mystery section, wrote *Jory* in 1978, following it with three sequels. He told me he intended a five-book western series—with the hero ending up a judge—but his publisher didn't want the character to age. A *Jory* motion picture came out in 1972.

BILL GULICK, LONGHORN WORDSMITH

Bill Gulick (1916–2013), longtime resident of Walla Walla, Washington, was christened Grover C. Gulick when he was born in Kansas City, Missouri. He called himself Bill as a college student, figuring it was more appealing to girls.

"By the time I was five years old, I was reading Zane Grey, pulp western magazines when I could get them, and all kinds of adult stories," Gulick said in *Sixty-Four Years as a Writer.*

Gulick decided to change his major at the University of Oklahoma from economics to writing and began marketing shoot-'em-up cowboy tales to *Ace-High Western, Dime Western* and other fiction magazines of the 1930s and '40s. His wife, Jeanne Abbott, whom he met at a community theater group, typed his manuscripts for years, until he finally broke down and acquired a word-processing computer.

The Gulicks rented a house on Swamp Road in Richmond in 1946–47. Gulick explained in response to my inquiry in 1985:

> *It was something of an accident that we were in that part of the country. I had taken my wife, who was born and raised in Tacoma, Wash., to New York City to show her what life was like in Greenwich Village, where I had spent nine months as a bachelor a few years earlier. After looking three weeks for a place we could afford, without finding it, we answered an ad in a Village paper put in by John and Margaret Grombach, wanting a responsible renter for an old farmhouse they had just remodeled in the Berkshires.*
>
> *We enjoyed our stay there and I got a lot of good writing done. It was there that I first cracked* The Saturday Evening Post, *which in those days was the goal of many writers.*

Gulick went on to write sixteen western and historical novels. He was active with Western Writers of America. Among his books made into motion pictures was *The Hallelujah Trail.*

CLAY PERRY AND JOHN L.E. PELL'S *HELL'S ACRES*

Never mind westerns, Berkshire claims a rip-snortin' eastern! It was a team effort.

John Legett Everett Pell (1876–1970) attended Sedgwick Institute in Great Barrington. He became a broker on the New York Produce Exchange. He was an interior decorator with Bertine & Co.; clients included the Aspinwall Hotel in Lenox. He was an assistant sales manager with Gryphon Tire & Rubber. Turning to writing, Pell scripted the silent movie *Down to the Sea in Ships* in the 1920s. Portions of the film are still screened daily at the Whaling Museum in New Bedford. He was chief historical research editor for movie director D.W. Griffith. He made educational films and worked for NBC radio.

With Clair W. "Clay" Perry (1887–1961), Pell wrote *Hell's Acres*, an adventure of horse thieves in Boston Corner, the southeastern extremity of Mount Washington. Inaccessible from Massachusetts, Boston Corner was a no-man's land inhabited by horse thieves and outlaws. The infamous John Morrissy–"Yankee" Sullivan thirty-seven-round, bare-fisted prizefight was held here in October 1853, and in embarrassment, Massachusetts gave the corner to New York within a few months.

As Pell and Perry, who spent three years on research, explain in a foreword, the novel is "based upon history which has never been published save in fragments appearing in old newspapers and in scattered and forgotten documents of the courts, town, state and national records, buried in the musty archives of historical libraries and collections—and retained in the memories of the few persons yet living who are able to recall the times."

Wisconsin-born Perry lived in Pittsfield and Cheshire. He wrote for the *Springfield Republican* and the *Berkshire Eagle*. An avid spelunker (he coined the term), his *Underground New England* (1939) is a treasure to cave explorers. Perry wrote stories for *Thrilling Adventures*, *Top-Notch*, *North West Romances* and the like. His novel *Heart of Hemlock* (1920) is about the wood pulp industry. He also wrote *The Phantom Forest* and *Roving River* (1921). Perry headed the WPA Writers' Project in Berkshire County during the Great Depression.

Perry and Pell collaborated on *The Canada Doctor* (1932) before writing *Hell's Acres*. Subtitled "A Historical Novel of the Wild East in the '50s," *Hell's Acres* is about Derek Wilkes, who infiltrates the Black Brant gang of horse thieves. He faces Spike Brant, scion of the outlaw leader, who has returned from the Bowery with devious plans. Wilkes falls in love with Jean Randall, whose father lost his farm to the rascal Black Brant. Members of a Dutch vigilante society plan to clean up the thieving gang, and Wilkes is their agent. He discovers the whereabouts of the Blow Hole, a tunnel-like trail through the mountains used to transport horses from New York to Massachusetts.

Perry persuaded burly Pittsfield cider maker Charlie Daniels to grow a beard and pose for a photo as Black Brant, the saloonkeeper. But the publisher thought it too scary and didn't include it in the book, according to the writer.

Perry may have loved the outdoors, but he couldn't navigate Boston Corner. Seeking the east entrance to the Blow Hole—a ravine reputed to be the historical hideaway of horse thieves—in winter 1938, four days after *Hell's Acres* came out, Perry disappeared. He turned up the next day, with a lame leg from falling on slippery snow. He'd taken refuge in an empty cabin and hobbled out below Mount Riga. He was embarrassed. But any publicity is good publicity, right?

Romance Writers

The Berkshires is ripe for romance.

Jean Webster, actual name Alice Jane Chandler Webster (1876–1916), was a great-niece of Samuel L. Clemens on her mother's side. Her father was Clemens's business manager. Webster and her husband, Glenn Ford McKinney, summered at Orchard House in Tyringham, and she wrote *Daddy Long Legs* (1912), the story of an orphan girl who grows up not knowing who her secret benefactor is. She wove Tyringham scenes into the background of the epistolary book. The best-remembered film version features Fred Astaire and Leslie Caron.

Nancy Thayer (b. 1943) writes sophisticated stories of families and relationships and romances. She was a Williamstown resident when her third novel, *Bodies and Souls*, came out in 1983. Set in a small New England town, it followed the lives of eight people. Earlier books were *Three Women at the Water's Edge* (1981) and *Stepping* (1980). Later ones were *Nell* (1985) and *Belonging* (1995). "The power of Thayer's novels—gentle and unpretentious, but nonetheless compelling—lies in the fact that the women within them, like the woman who wrote them, all choose to enter the tunnel. Like Thayer herself, the characters, who sometimes stride and sometimes limp from one chapter to the next, understand that life is a responsibility—one that they're willing to embrace," Eileen Kuperschmid wrote. Thayer now lives on Nantucket.

Jane M. Claypool (b. 1933), a longtime Pittsfield resident, wrote dozens of romances and other books for juveniles and young adults. *A Love for Violet*

(1982), typically, is about a shy girl from a big family who is shunned by the popular crowd at school. She ends up falling in love with a football hero who asks her to the prom. A book for unenthusiastic readers, *Choices* (1980), written as Jane Miner, includes photos of Hancock Shaker Village, Great Barrington Fair and other local scenes. Claypool has also used the pen name "Veronica Ladd." Born in Texas, the writer taught English, art, social studies and science in California, New Jersey and Pittsfield. She was named Writer of the Year in 1981 by the Society of Children's Book Writers. In 1989, she founded the Center for Spiritual Living in California, where she now lives.

Interestingly, the Berkshirite who wrote the most romance stories was a man...

BILL SEVERN'S RANGELAND ROMANCES

I spotted the stack of old magazines in the secondhand bookstore. I'm not a regular reader of *Rangeland Romances*, you should know. But I brought home three issues because they carried stories by Bill Severn.

William L. Severn (1914–1992) took naturally to writing, as his father was a newspaper executive in New York City. Severn worked for Transradio Press Service and later the *Buffalo Evening News* and Associated Press. Journalism was his day job. "Meanwhile, I was writing articles and short stories on the side," he explained. "It built up enough so that I went to full-time freelance writing."

He found regular markets with *Love Story* and *Ranch Romances*. Some issues carried stories with his byline and others by "Lillian Lane" or "Sarah Graham" when more than one of his yarns appeared in the same issue.

"My first pulp story went to *Ranch Romances*," he said.

> *"Together in Taos," it was called. That was in 1940–41. I sold pretty well my first year. I had been trying for five to ten years without selling. It was a big day when my first story landed.*
>
> *I had a standing deal with Harry Widmer, the editor at* Popular *for* Romantic Western, *and with Daisy Bacon at [Street & Smith's]* Love Story *magazine. I did 20,000 words a month, a 10,000-word novelette and two stories...*
>
> *I once had six pulp cover stories on the stands at one time. I wasn't ashamed of them. It took damn good craftsmanship to write for the pulps.*

Severn sold stories to *Liberty, Country Gentleman, Collier's* and *Seventeen*. But the quality magazines, while offering more prestige and money, were often slower to pay.

His nonfiction includes young adult books about the Roaring Twenties and Capitol Hill pages and more than twenty-five books about another keen interest, magicians and magic.

Severn lived in Sheffield in the early 1960s when he was advertising manager for the *Lakeville Journal*. By 1980, when he discussed his writing with me, he had a home off Silver Street in Great Barrington. Severn and his wife, Susan, later moved to Lee.

After waiting all those years to find Bill Severn romance stories, did I read them? You bet. "Kiss Me

Bill Severn wrote dozens of books about magic—and hundreds of cowgirl romances. *Bernard A. Drew, 1982.*

Good-By, Cowboys!" in the January 1947 *Rangeland Romances* is about sassy Sallie Gibson, who doesn't believe any of the Texas trail herders are serious in their wooing...until she meets Dane Coleman.

SCIENCE FICTION, FANTASY AND HORROR WRITERS

Great Barrington native W.E.B. Du Bois (1868–1963)—the educator, editor and advocate for social justice—was Berkshire's first writer of futuristic fiction? Yes. An early and vigorous champion of civil rights, the bulk of his writing was nonfiction. But his short story "The Comet" (1920), which depicts the relationship between a black man and a white woman of means—the last two people on a post-apocalyptic planet—was included in *Darkwater: Voices From Within the Veil* (1920). It was reprinted in the anthology *Dark Matter* (2000). Also in *Darkwater* was Du Bois' "Jesus Christ in Texas," in which Christ returns as an enslaved black man in Texas destined to set his people free.

W.E.B. Du Bois, left; his wife, Nina; and James Weldon Johnson in 1928 celebrated the gift of his grandfather's old homestead in Great Barrington by NAACP friends. *Special Collections and Archives, W.E.B. Du Bois Library, University of Massachusetts–Amherst.*

Du Bois's childhood homesite on Route 23 in Great Barrington is a National Historic Landmark park maintained by the University of Massachusetts at Amherst.

John Crowley (b. 1942), recipient of the World Fantasy Award for Live Achievement (2006), wrote the dystopian *Little, Big* in 1981. Crowley lived in Tyringham beginning in 1977. His other novels include *The Deep, Beasts, Engine Summer* and *Ægypt* (1987), the last an exploration of the world's secret history encoded in myth.

Paul Park (b. 1954) of North Adams began writing humanist science fiction/fantasy with *The Starbridge Chronicles* in 1987. His recent book is *All Those Vanished Engines* (2014). He teaches at Williams College.

Isobel Noble of North Egremont launched the Ruin fantasy trilogy in 2008. It's about a utopian settlement in the Rocky Mountains in the aftermath of a nuclear disaster.

Gabriel Squailia of Pittsfield brings the non-living to life in *Dead Boys* (2015), a genre-crossing tale of zombies on a quest.

Anton Strout, once of Dalton, has completed two urban fantasy trilogies. The first features Simon Canderous (beginning in 2008), a reformed thief and psychometrist; the second is about Alexandra Belarus (beginning in 2012), who has discovered her family's secret ability to bring stone to life.

If Du Bois is a surprise in this section, what about Edith Wharton? Her eleven paranormal magazine stories were collected in *Ghosts* (1937). "If it sends a cold shiver down one's spine," the author says in the preface, "it has done its job and done it well."

ANTHONY M. RUD'S EERIE "OOZE"

Anthony Rud (1893–1942)—his middle name was Melville—turned in the cover story for America's legendary fantasy magazine *Weird Tales*. "Ooze" greeted purchasers of that first issue, dated March 1923.

The future scribe graduated from Dartmouth in 1914 but abandoned plans to study at Rush Medical College. "His father was a doctor, and wanted him to become a doctor," the writer's son, Anthony G. Rud Sr., explained to me in 1983. "But he hated dissecting and that sort of thing and quit school. I think he wanted to get married."

Rud sold his first novel, *The Second Generation*, to Doubleday in 1923. Based on his father's experiences as a Norwegian emigrant, the book was well received. He became part of the Chicago circle that included playwrights Ben Hecht, Charles MacArthur and Sherwood Anderson. Rud moved to New York the same year he wrote "Ooze." He became an editor with Doubleday Page. He wrote westerns *Devil's Heirloom* (1924)

Anthony M. Rud's classic "Ooze" was the cover story for the first issue of *Weird Tales* in 1923. *Hubert Rogers/courtesy Anthony G. Rud.*

and *Last Grubstake* (1925). In 1927, he became editor of *Adventure*, the prestigious pulp magazine.

"It was a pretty good paying job," the writer's son said, "and he got to meet people like Gene Tunney and Mae West." After two years, Rud returned to freelancing for *Argosy*, *Lariat* and other pulps. He did editorial work for *Detective Story Magazine*. His cowboy novels include *The Last Grubstake* (1924) and *Sentence of the Six Gun* (1926).

Rud found a steady market with *Detective Fiction Weekly* (*DFW*) and resurrected a detective he had created for a story in *Green Book* in 1918, Jigger Masters. The Masters stories were, well, unusual. In *The Rose Bath Riddle*, the private detective solves a series of murders on a Long Island estate—one by the curious method of freezing the victim in a scalding shower. Rud drew on his earlier studies of medicine and anatomy to make the preposterous sound feasible. In *The Stuffed Men*, bodies are found with their insides turned to straw. *House of the Damned* was a third Masters serial, companion to a dozen short stories for *DFW*, until the editor decided to move on to another character. The last Masters story, "The Encyclopedia Murders," was in the magazine's May 15, 1937 issue.

Rud; his wife, Elizabeth; and their three children beginning in 1937 rented a house six months of the year in Sheffield, first on Rannapo Road and then on Undermountain Road.

Anthony M. Rud died of a heart attack in New York in 1942.

"Ooze" has been reprinted several times in the decades since.

"It isn't great literature," his son admitted of Rud's pulp writing, "but it has a certain knack which not everyone has."

YULE LIKE THIS

Christmas is a literary genre, isn't it?

Unitarian minister Edmund Hamilton Sears (1810–1876), the Sandisfield native who penned the words to the beloved carol "It Came Upon a Midnight Clear" (1849), wrote other Noels that few know the words to, much less the tune. "A Christmas Song," for example, was first published in the *Boston Observer* in 1824. It begins, "Calm on the listening ear of night."

Joan Ackermann of Mill River, co-founder of Mixed Company Theater in Great Barrington, inspired by background characters from the carol "Good King Wenceslas," wrote the Christmas musical *Yonder Peasant* in 1987. The characters were raucous and adorable. The set was a treehouse, the theater filled with the scent of pine.

"When you write a play," Ackermann told *Playbill*, "you get completely transported into another world. You're in a whole other realm. Obsessed."

Ackermann also wrote *Don't Ride the Clutch*, *Bed and Breakfast* and *Stanton's Garage*. *Zara Spook and Other Lures* ran off-Broadway in 1990. She wrote scripts for the TV show *Arli$$. Q W E R T Y: Typewriter Plays* premiered in 2013. Shakespeare & Company commissioned *Ice Glen* and staged it at the Spring Lawn estate. "I think people are really sort of a crop of the land where they come from," the playwright told Louise Kennedy. "Place is always important."

Ackermann and her Mixed Company co-artistic director Gillian Seidl have taken her work to the Edinburgh Fringe Festival in Scotland and to the Humana Festival of New American Plays in Louisville, Kentucky, where in 1996 she debuted *Off the Map* (which she turned into a screenplay for a film directed by Campbell Scott in 2003).

Clergyman and hymnist Washington Gladden (1836–1918) penned a Berkshire Yule story, "The Strange Adventures of a Wood-Sled," for the December 1879 *St. Nicholas* magazine. It describes the harrowing trip home to Pittsfield for Christmas made by the Burnhams and their children, their train ride through the town of Washington and their encounter with a white-bearded sled driver.

Willard Douglas Coxey (1861–1943) wrote a sixteen-stanza verse, "How the Kiddies Saved Old Santa Claus," for the *Berkshire Courier* in 1931. The Egremonter also penned two volumes of Indian and other legends, *Romances of Old Berkshire* (1931) and *Ghosts of Old Berkshire* (1934).

Joan Ackermann of Mill River has established herself as a writer of vibrant plays. *Tina Sotis.*

Richard Chase Mears (b. 1935) left a career in investment and advertising to run Whistler's Inn in Lenox. He has written for adults (*Anubis Rex*, 2003) and teens (*The Bard Club*, 2014), but his *Saint Nick and the Space Nicks* (2004)—in which Santa helps a Venusian counterpart finish delivering toys—is for young readers.

Clement Clarke Moore (1779–1863) never made it to Berkshire. But his desk did. The son of an Episcopal bishop who owned a manor along the Hudson River in New York City, Moore is said to have composed his famed holiday verse "A Visit from St. Nicholas" for daughters Margaret and Charity in 1822, while sitting at a particular mahogany desk. Moore willed the desk to Harriet Butler of Troy, New York. She left it to a cousin. It came into the possession of Blanche Crane Austin Rockhill in 1928, and she brought it to her Boulders property on Maple Avenue in Great Barrington, where it remained for about ten years. It has been at the New York Historical Society since 1956.

Shake, Shake, Shakers

Fiction writers have been curious about Shaker communities such as the one in Hancock, and sometimes they've been openly disdainful.

Charles Dickens (1812–1870) toured the United States before he crafted his 1843 story of Scrooge and Tiny Tim and wrote in *American Notes* (1832), "I so abhor, and from my soul detest that bad spirit, no matter by what class or sect it may be entertained, which would strip life of its healthful graces, rob youth of its innocent pleasures, pluck from maturity and age their pleasant ornaments, and make existence but a narrow path towards the grave." Dickens called on the Shakers at New Lebanon, New York, in June 1842. Or at least, he tried to; they wouldn't let him in.

Harriet Martineau (1802–1876), the English-born novelist and children's writer, was also wary of Shakers. The guest of Catharine Sedgwick in Stockbridge for six weeks in 1834, she visited the Shakers at New Lebanon and Hancock and, while appreciative of their industries and hard work, found their way of life too much labor and no joy. She scoffed at their celibacy.

Josh Billings explained how the celibacy worked: "The Shakers dont marry. If young Shakers fall in luv tha are sot tu weeding onions, and that kures them forthwithly."

Other writers have been more measured and sympathetic.

Robert W. McCulloch (1867–1946) studied the Shaker settlements at Mount Lebanon and Hancock for a quarter of a century before writing a novel about their lifestyle, *Me and Thee* (1937). McCulloch, a Southfield resident for twenty years, worked for the Associated Press and for the *Evening Telegram* and *Evening Mail*.

Dramatist, public relations consultant and innkeeper Philip Barber (1903–1981) composed a Shaker music-drama, *The Passionate Quest* (1969). Based on Shaker history researched by Walter Wilson, it was read at Berkshire Playhouse and staged by Berkshire Lyric Theatre at the Berkshire Museum. Barber taught playwriting at Yale and became a screenwriter for MGM. Barber's drama *I, Elizabeth Otis* was produced in 1968. He purchased Wheatleigh in Stockbridge in 1950, and he and his wife, Stephanie, established the legendary Music Inn there. Barber later lived in Becket.

The Hancock Shaker community during the Great Depression figures in the 2001 novel *Killing Gifts*, the fifth of the Sister Rose Callahan mysteries by Deborah Woodworth (b. 1949) of Minnesota. A young woman has been found strangled in the Sisters' Summerhouse in deep winter. Eldress Rose of Kentucky is called to the City of Peace and, with her friend Gennie Malone, solves the crime.

Rachel Urquhart's novel *The Visionist* (2013) follows fifteen-year-old Polly Kimball, who is taken in by the Shakers at the (fictional) City of Hope (modeled after Hancock) after she set fire to her home. She is considered a mystic. She befriends Charity, a Shaker sister who has grown up in the village. Simon Pryor is a detective investigating the fire. The author has often summered at her family's converted Shaker meetinghouse in Tyringham. Her grandfather was playwright Sidney Howard.

An authentic Shaker voice, Sister Fidella E. Estabrook (d. 1910) of Hancock Shaker Village wrote a book of spiritual verse, *Berkshire Wild Flowers*, published in 1902. "Morning Thoughts" begins: "Awake, my soul, to the music,/That pulses the earth this morn!/To the merry jubilant chorus,/That heralds the beautiful dawn!"

VIII

FOR YOUNGER READERS

BOYS' AND GIRLS' HARDCOVER SERIES BOOKS

At the turn of the twentieth century, publishers decided young adults merited their own (diluted) literature. Thus emerged the hardcover series. You've already met Nancy Drew in the Mystery section. Here are a few others.

Laura Dent Crane's juvenile hardcover novel *The Automobile Girls in the Berkshires* (1910) was the second of six books with the young heroines.

> *A crimson automobile was climbing the steep inclines of the Berkshire Hills. Now it rose to the crest of a road. Again it dipped into a valley. It looked like a scarlet autumn leaf blown down from one of the giant forest trees that guarded the slopes of the mountains.*
>
> *Mollie Thurston stood up in the back of the motor car, waving a long green veil.*
>
> *"Isn't the scenery just too perfect for words?" she called to Ruth.*

There's no information about the writer Crane, nor about another writer, Isabel Hornibrook, whose *Camp Fire Girls and Mount Greylock* came out in 1917. In this story, Phyllis Grayson, Olive and Sybil Deering and other Camp Fire Sisters "journey to the loftier ranges of the Berkshire Hills." The author describes Mount Greylock Reservation and The Hopper. Her characters enjoy 347 pages of adventures and are sorry to say goodbye.

The Motor Girls Through New England (1911), partially set in the Berkshires, was one of several hardcover series books by "Margaret Penrose," a house name for the Stratemeyer fiction syndicate.

Percy Kees Fitzhugh (1876–1950) was real enough. His boys' books featuring Tom Slade, Westy Martin and Pee-Wee Harris include *Roy Blakesley on the Mohawk Trail* (1925). The boys take a road trip. "So then we were in the Berkshires—we were in Great Barrington. Gee whiz, I don't know why they call it *great*. It wasn't so great. But anyway it was dark when we went through it," blasphemes one character.

Owen Johnson (1878–1952), the son of Robert Underwood Johnson, made his first story sale at age six to *St. Nicholas*. He founded and edited the Lawrenceville Preparatory School literary magazine. After receiving his degree from Yale, Johnson wrote humorous juvenile novels, including *The Tennessee Shad* (1911) and *Stover at Yale* (1911). His Lawrenceville stories found a new audience, thanks to a 1987 *American Playhouse* television dramatization of the schooldays of Gutter Pup, the Uncooked Beefsteak, Old Ironsides, Doc and Dink Stover. The stories, which appeared in the *Saturday Evening Post*, have a droll humor yet sophisticated voice. The characters fall in age and disposition somewhere between Booth Tarkington's Penrod and P.G. Wodehouse's Bertie Wooster. *The Prodigious Hickey*, typically, is about a new student who bests the pancake-eating record at Conover's restaurant and earns free pancakes for all the students for a day.

Johnson bought an estate near the Stockbridge Golf Club called Ingleside in 1922. He was an avid golfer and supporter of the Berkshire Playhouse as well as the New York Philharmonic concerts at the Hanna Farm in Interlaken. The writer moved to Florida in 1948.

The first of Walter Prichard Eaton's ten scouting books issued from 1912 to 1934, *The Boy Scouts of Berkshire*, follows the Chipmunk Patrol of "Southmead" as its members hike to Massachusetts's highest peak. "From Cheshire they planned to walk up the carriage road to the top of Greylock," we read, "descend into North Adams by the Ravine trail, go over Hoosac Mountain, beneath which the famous tunnel is bored, tramp up the hills north of the Deerfield River through the little town of Rowe."

It took fourteen days (and sixteen pages) to make the 150 miles.

THE BOB'S HILL BOYS IN ADAMS

Mount Greylock, Peck's Falls and other locations in Adams inspired the writer of the Bob's Hill Boys books, Charles Pierce Burton (1862–1947).

The author was the son of Adams native Nellie Lapham and her husband, Pierce Burton, a reporter with the North Adams *Transcript*. His mother died soon after his birth, so Charles was raised by his grandparents, Mr. and

Juliette Wilk-Chaffee, left, shows visitors sites in Adams that provided settings for Charles Pierce Burton's Bob's Hill Boys series books. *Bernard A. Drew, 2006.*

Mrs. George Lapham, who lived on Park Street, next door to state senator Theodore R. Plunkett.

Young Burton left Adams in 1874 when his father remarried and moved to Aurora, Illinois, to work in the print trade. Charles rose from printer's devil to reporter to publisher of the Aurora *Daily Express*, which his father established in 1882. He later was editor and publisher of the *Aurora Herald*. Then for two decades he edited *The Earth Mover*, a construction magazine issued by the Austin-Western Machinery Co., maker of road graders and street sweepers. He wrote occasional articles for *Harper's*.

Approached by an editorial syndicate agent, Burton put to paper the imagined childhood adventures he'd been relating to his grandchildren. Holt brought out *The Boys of Bob's Hill* in 1905. This book and sequels make remarkable use of the north Berkshire setting.

"I have served an apprenticeship in that best of all schools for writers—newspaper work—and naturally was ambitious to see my stuff in book form," Burton told an Aurora *Beacon-News* reporter in 1928.

The gang takes its name from Bob's Hill, the prominence behind Adams Town Hall. This is how Burton described it for the *Beacon-News* in 1934: "Park Street, where the old home stood, skirts the foot of a large hill which was a favorite playground for us village boys. Sixty years and more ago, that hill was called Bob's Hill because at one time it belonged to Robert Briggs."

The stories are in the Tom Sawyer vein—the gang explore the woods, pretend they are outlaws, discover a cave, frighten girls, fight off a rival Gingham Ground Gang, inadvertently start a fire at a picnic, discover a treasure and help an elderly woman.

This is from *The Boy Scouts of Bob's Hill* (1912):

> *Over the brow of* [Bob's] *hill and a little south are Plunkett's woods. West, straight back, a mile or more, begins the timbered slope of old Greylock, which, everybody knows, is the highest mountain in Massachusetts. And in the edge of the first woods, a little back from the road* [West Road], *is the prettiest place you ever sat eyes upon. Grown-up folks call it "the glen," but we boys just say "Peck's Falls." I don't know why, only there is a waterfall there, which begins in a brook, somewhere up on the mountainside, and plays and tumbles along, until finally it pours down from a high cliff into a pool a hundred feet below; then dashes off to join Hoosac River.*

Teacher and historian Juliette Wilk-Chaffee offered to show me Burton's town landmarks. When she taught at Plunkett Elementary

School, she said, "For many years I would guide the students from my classes on a tour of Adams that highlighted the places where the boys staged their adventures. We would pause along the trip and quote from the book and read descriptions of the places where we were standing over 100 years later."

We met in front of Adams Memorial Library. Across the street was where the Old Elm once stood—it's where messages were concealed in the Burton books.

"Burton was writing about post–Civil War Adams," Wilk-Chaffee explained, "when the town was going through dynamic industrial growth."

It was the era of Plunkett textile factories and Brown paper mills.

As we walked along Park Street, Wilk-Chaffee explained the narrator of the boys' adventures, John Alexander Smith, aka Pedro, is a loosely disguised Burton. Pedro served as secretary for the Bob's Hill Boys as his handwriting was most difficult to read—thus their doings would be kept secret. The old Union Hotel building and a handful of other Park Street buildings, greatly changed now, were there in Burton's day.

The Gingham Ground—where another gang of boys held fort—was Renfrew Field north of the village. Burton's name for it came from the factory there that produced gingham cloth.

Industrialist Charles T. Plunkett razed the Lapham home in 1908 and built a new mansion. The mansion later became home to the American Legion post and is now Adams Town Hall. Next door, where Greylock Federal Credit Union is today, stood W.C. Plunkett's mansion called Monrath.

From the Ashuwillticook Rail Trail, a remnant of the old railroad line from Pittsfield, we saw the Hoosac River—channeled in the 1950s for flood control, but a natural river in the days of the Bob's Hill Boys. It's gone now, but the old South Adams Academy where Pedro, Skinny and the others went to school was slightly behind and south of McDonald's, Wilk-Chaffee pointed out. We skirted Plunkett Woods (now Russell Field) and walked uphill to Forest Park Country Club.

"The ninth hole was a popular sledding spot," our guide said. We walked onto a dirt road into the golf course because at the top of the knoll were the Bob's Hill Boys' twin stones. The stones are gone—taken out to improve the golf course years ago.

We climbed West Mountain Road, and Wilk-Chaffee took us to the unmarked entrance to a woods trail on the right. Directly downhill on a side trail are lower Peck's Falls and Pulpit Rock. The Bob's Hill Boys favored the secret caves below the falls; in one of the tales, smoke from their fire in one of the caves seeped up through the ground and startled adults who picnicked above. The real caves were wiped out in the flooding of 1901, Wilk-Chaffee said.

CHILDREN'S AND YOUNG ADULT BOOKS

We'll look at the next collection of writers as a child might—in no discernible order.

Elizabeth Winthrop, daughter of political journalist Stewart Alsop, a great-grandniece of Theodore Roosevelt and a part-time Williamstown resident, found a wide young adult readership for *The Castle in the Attic* (1994) and its sequel, *The Battle for the Castle* (1994). *Dear Mr. President: Franklin Delano Roosevelt, Letters from a Mill Town Girl* (2001) is about Emma Bortoletti, daughter of Italian immigrants living in North Adams, and her (fictional) correspondence with FDR during the time of the Great Depression. She talks about her family's daily life. He talks about ideas he has for recovery programs. Another of the author's sixty books is *Counting on Grace* (2008), based on a Lewis Hine photo of a twelve-year-old French-Canadian mill girl. It examines issues related to child labor and family hardships.

Illustrator and author Jan Brett (b. 1949) summers in Tyringham. She is known for *The Wild Christmas Reindeer* (1990), which appeared on the *New York Times* bestseller list; *The Mitten*; *The Owl and the Pussycat*; *Town Mouse, Country Mouse*; and *Trouble with Trolls*.

Barbara Shook Hazen (b. 1930) of Otis has written more than two dozen children's books, including

Elizabeth Winthrop of Williamstown imagined Franklin D. Roosevelt as a pen pal. *Jennifer Mardus/courtesy Elizabeth Winthrop.*

Alone at Home (1992), about a girl who wants to babysit herself, and *Turkey in the Straw* (1993), which dramatizes the popular folk song. Early on, she wrote *Mr. Ed, the Talking Horse* in 1958, based on the popular television series.

James L. Ford (1854–1928), longtime literary critic for the *New York Herald*, attended the Reed-Hoffmann School in Stockbridge and fictionalized his experiences in *Dr. Dodd's School* (1892).

Roni Schotter (b. 1946) has written some thirty books for children, among them *Bunny's Night Out* (1989), published when she lived in West Stockbridge.

Veteran journalist Ruth Bass (b. 1934) of Richmond wrote *Sarah's Daughter* (2007), the story of fourteen-year-old Rose Hibbard raising her siblings in a household without a mother but with an alcoholic father. The setting is the nineteenth century. A sequel, *Rose* (2010), follows the heroine's quest to become a teacher.

Alice Schick and Joel Schick (b. 1945) shared their Monterey farmhouse with six cats, a dog and a family of gerbils as they wrote and illustrated children's books such as Joel Schick's *Christmas Present* (1977), James Whitcomb Riley's poem "Little Orphant Annie" and *The Gobble-Uns'll Git You Ef You Don't Watch Out!* (1975). Joel Schick was also an authorized Sesame Street book artist. Alice Schick's books include *Kongo and Kumba: Two Gorillas*, *The Peregrine Falcons* (1975) and *The Siamang Gibbons: An Ape Family*. The Schicks now live in California.

It's not mentioned by name, but Great Barrington's Mason Library stands in for the Sesame Street Library in Tom Leigh's illustrations for *Grover's Book of Cute Little Baby Animals* (1980) by B.G. Ford. Leigh lived in Sheffield at the time.

Stockbridge transplants Molly (1896–1985) and Norman Rockwell (1894–1978) collaborated on *Willie Was Different: The Tale of an Ugly Thrushing* (1969) for young readers. Norman Rockwell illustrated the story of droopy-winged, pigeon-toed Willie, different from others of his species and something of a rebel. The story first appeared in *McCall's*. Berkshire House Publishers in 1995 reissued the book but in the version Norman wrote before Molly revised it. Norman was born in New York City. Molly (née Punderson) was a Stockbridge native.

The first of Pittsfielder Ty Allan Jackson's books for young readers, *Danny Dollar Millionaire Extraordinaire: The Lemonade Escapade* (2010), is a story about small business and African American children.

"I became an author in part because of the lack of diversity in children's books," the Bronx native told me.

Ty Allan Jackson of Pittsfield writes books for young readers. *Courtesy Ty Allan Jackson.*

Since 2012 less than 7 percent of the children's books feature a diverse character and the few that do exist are often cultural or historical, not simply fun books that feature children of color. As my son once phrased it, "Why do I have to read about Dr. Martin Luther King? My friends don't read about John F. Kennedy."

All of my books feature a diverse cast of characters and a protagonist who just happens to be African American. There is nothing topical about my books; they are just fun, entertaining books that every child can read and enjoy.

The Supadupa Kid (2012), also for ages six to twelve, offers the exploits of Javon Williams, newly endowed with superpowers, as he faces Hoody the bully. Dot, the main character in *When I Close My Eyes* (2011), exercises her imagination. The book is for early readers.

Jackson received the first Martin Luther King Jr. Content of Character Award from Massachusetts governor Deval Patrick in 2012.

RACHEL FIELD'S HITTY

Berkshire's most prominent writer of juvenile books spent ten childhood years in Stockbridge, where, she said, "I learned to like below-zero weather and to find all sorts of growing wild things, such as arbutus in spring, wild strawberries in summer and fringed gentians in early fall."

Rachel Lyman Field (1894–1942) was the daughter of Dr. Matthew Dickinson Field Jr. and Lucy Atwater Field, great-niece of David Dudley Field Jr. and Cyrus Field. She lived in the Old Corner House on Main Street with her widowed mother.

She attended Radcliffe and wrote synopses for a silent film company. She married literary agent Arthur Pederson. She wrote books for young readers, including *Eliza and the Elves* (1925), *Calico Bush* (1931), *The Magic Pawn Shop: A New Year's Eve Fantasy* (1927) and *Little Dog Toby* (1946). She wrote the English lyrics to the version of Franz Schubert's "Ave Maria" used in the Walt Disney film *Fantasia* (1943).

Her biggest hit with readers of all ages is *Hitty: Her First Hundred Years* (1929), illustrated by Dorothy P. Lathrop, which tells the story of a doll that travels everywhere with young Phoebe Preble. The book earned the Newbery Medal from the American Library Association. A revised edition by Rosemary Wells (b. 1943) came out in 2000.

Field won the National Book Award in 1930 for *Time Out of Mind* and wrote the Caldecott Medal–winning *Prayer for a Child* (1944).

The Stockbridge Library Historical Room owns the original doll, carved from white ash, and the annotated typescript, as well as Field's letters. Hitty was the gift of Roger Linscott, a descendant of Lathrop. "The nice thing for us is that we already had an extensive collection on the Field family," Historical Room curator Barbara Allen told reporter Shelly Jarenski, "so to have Rachel Field's doll come to us gave us the chance to fill that collection and to display several elements in the making of a book."

The Historical Room has sponsored gatherings for Hitty fans—and afforded the opportunity to those who have crafted their own versions of the doll to have its picture taken alongside the actual Hitty.

Hitty is probably the No. 2 attraction at the Stockbridge Library Historical Room, according to Barbara Allen, right after theologian Jonathan Edwards and before the Stockbridge Indians.

IX

HUMORISTS AND CARTOONISTS

Josh Billings Milked His Audience

The yellowed scrap of paper bears a message written in a bold hand in dark brown ink: "Thare iz only 2 advantages that i kan see in going too the Devil, one is, you kant miss the way, and the other is, you are sure to git thare—." It could only be a quotation by Josh Billings, and that's how it's signed. Ephemera of undeniable Berkshire connection, I took it home from an antiquarian book fair.

Lanesboro-born Henry Wheeler Shaw (1818–1885) was a traveling wag and cracker-box philosopher of his day. Gifted from the cradle with a keen wit, he eventually made it a paying profession. Shaw swam in Pontoosuc Lake as a boy, played practical jokes with the Lanesboro church bell and attempted scholarly pursuits in Lenox. He departed Hamilton College after attending only a year (expelled for swiping the clapper from the chapel bell) and at his father's suggestion headed west. In 1845, he returned to Lanesboro long enough to marry Zilpha Bradford. They farmed for a few seasons and then, when Shaw's family was two children strong in 1858, they moved to Poughkeepsie, New York, and he became a real estate agent and auctioneer.

Shaw began his writing career at age forty-five with "Essa on the Muel bi Josh Billings" (1860). He "sprang suddenly into fame as a wit and philosopher of unique expressions in his writings and lectures," Clay Perry wrote.

Lanesboro native Henry Wheeler Shaw called himself Josh Billings for his comedic almanacs and essays. *Sarony/author's collection.*

Shaw said he chose his pen name from an old friend whom he admired greatly, Josh Crenaw. "But somehow the latter name didn't jingle, so to speak, with the former." So he went with "Billings."

The humorist's first book, *Josh Billings: His Book of Sayings* (1865), contained aphorisms such as: "Poverty is the only birthright that a man can't lose" and "Life consists not in holding good cards but in playing those you do hold well."

For over a decade, 1869–80, Billings produced annual *Farmer's Allminax* parodies. He kidded the weather forecasts, Zodiac pronouncements, planting schedules and so on. Here's one of his January horoscopes: "The young man born this month will remain a bachelor until his 16th year, and will have curly hair." For February, "The young female born during this month will show great judgment in sorting her lovers, and will finally marry a real estate agent."

Billings was a favorite of Presidents Abraham Lincoln and Chester A. Arthur, who invited the josher to dine at the White House in 1884.

Shaw returned frequently to his hometown and neighboring New Ashford. He also visited Pittsfield and Stockbridge, in the latter town staying with Landlord Plumb at the Red Lion Inn. Billings prattled about "Milk" at a fundraiser for Hope Fire Company in Great Barrington in 1869. The town's newspaper observed Billings's striking bearing:

> *More than two yards tall; is somewhat round-shouldered, and sports a mustache about as large as a gobble turkey's wings. From his looks, one would scarcely expect to find him the comical critter that he is, although he has an oddity of manner quite peculiar; but his style of delivery is most applicable to his humor…In many of his short sparkles of wit, there was an undercurrent of wisdom, and throughout the whole there was a deal of excellent philosophy.*

One dour outlander was disappointed with the program. He had come expecting guidance on scientific farming practices.

Billings's grave is in Center Cemetery in Lanesboro. His childhood homestead on Bridge Street was razed in 1962. A lion's head doorknocker was saved and is in the Berkshire Historical Society's collection. The property, including Constitution Hill, is maintained by Berkshire Natural Resources Council. A second family home, Hillcrest on Main Street, burned in 1974. The Josh Billings RunAground bicycling-paddling-running race has been held each September since 1976.

MARK TWAIN HAD A FRIGHT

"Mark Twain" had a mixed reception when he gave a talk at Sumner Hall in Great Barrington in October 1871, two years after publication of his first book, *The Innocents Abroad*. The *Berkshire Courier* termed his quips "rehash" and "stale" humor before "an audience of four hundred people, and as far as we have been able to learn, at least three hundred and ninety of them went away dissatisfied and disappointed."

A neophyte public speaker, Samuel Langhorne Clemens (1835–1910) was experimenting with his talks, according to letters he wrote to his wife, Olivia "Livy" Langdon Clemens. He would soon conquer both stage and bookstore.

Born in Missouri, he worked as printer and riverboat pilot, prospector and reporter. His tall tale "The Celebrated Frog of Calaveras County" was an early popular success. Later works include *The Adventures of Tom Sawyer* (1876), *Life on the Mississippi* (1883) and *The Adventures of Huckleberry Finn* (1884).

After his wife's death, Samuel Clemens summered as a guest of Richard Watson Gilder in Tyringham. *A.F. Bradley, 1907/Library of Congress.*

"Hot-tempered, profane, wreathed in tobacco smoke, enthralled by games and gadgets, extravagant, sentimental, superstitious, chivalrous to the point of the ridiculous—he was all these things," according to Stanley J. Kunitz and Howard Haycraft.

Clemens lived in Hartford, Connecticut, for nearly twenty years. In 1904, following the death of his wife while in Italy, the author sought out his friend Richard Watson Gilder (1844–1909), whose country home Four Brooks Farm was in the Berkshires. Gilder edited *Century Magazine* and wrote occasional poetry, including "Evening in Tyringham Valley."

Gilder's daughter Francesca Palmer recalled that Clemens cabled to ask if he could visit: "He felt the need of being near a friend after such a tragic loss. He was completely devoted and entirely dependent upon his wife and did not see how he could go on without her."

Clemens stepped from a train in Lee on the afternoon of July 20. Daughters Clara and Jean arrived within a week from Elmira, New York, where they had just buried their mother. The family butler, Clemens's secretary and servants were with them. Clara soon took ill and returned to New York.

"We went right to Tyringham…after the funeral," Clemens's housekeeper Katy Leary wrote. "We went there to be near the Gilders, and oh! it seemed kind of heavenly to get there with those lovely friends after them awful weeks of suffering. We stayed there all summer and Mr. Clemens got calmer, and went back and forth to New York and busied himself looking for a house for the winter."

In the quiet of the secluded Tyringham valley, Clemens penned the epitaph for his wife's monument: "Warm summer sun/Shine kindly here./Warm southern wind/Blow softly here./Green sod above/Lie light, lie light/Good night, dear heart,/Good night, good night."

Gilder's Glencote guest cottage at the corner of George Cannon Road was a frequent sanctuary of the literati. The same season as Twain, Alice Hegan Rice (1870–1942), author of *Mrs. Wiggs of the Cabbage Patch* (1901), and her husband, poet and dramatist Cale Young Rice (1872–1943), were also Gilder guests. Alice Rice said in her autobiography that Clemens had a "mane of snowy hair, his beetling eyebrows overhanging the bluest and most mischievous pair of eyes."

Clemens had a fright the day his daughter had an accident. Dr. J.J. Hassett in Lee thought the bruised and badly shaken patient brought to his door was "Julia Langdon." That's what she told rescuers after the horse she was riding was struck by a trolley car near the Pleasure Park on Route 102. The young woman sprained her ankle. She soon admitted to being Jean Clemens.

The twenty-four-year-old had gone for an evening horseback ride with Gilder's son Rodman. The *Berkshire Eagle* reported her horse backed onto the track just as the 10:15 p.m. trolley approached, and it spooked the animal. Clemens was covered with blood, from a cut by glass from one of the trolley's windows and from a nosebleed. Motorman Charles Walker and conductor Sanford Jones quickly took her aboard and rushed her into town. Gilder identified Clemens with a false name and said he was "Joseph Drake." Although some may have recognized her, it was later explained that Gilder, believing her more seriously injured than she really was, didn't want word of her accident to get back to her sister in New York before she had a chance to send a telegram.

Arrival at Glencote of a bandaged daughter surely did little for her father's composure.

The Clemens family's visit long remained in the memories of residents. The author gave Lee papermaker Wellington Smith an autographed note, for example: "Don't use your morals week days—It's apt to get 'em out of repair for Sundays. Yours truly, Mark Twain."

The humorist presented Herbert E. Moore, superintendent of Gilder's Four Brooks Farm, with a full set of twenty-three volumes of his works. Moore also kept one of the aluminum horseshoes from Jean Clemens's ill-fated mount. He nailed it over his door—did he consider it an emblem of good luck?

Gilder's newlywed neighbor Grace Henop Tytus and her husband, Robb de Peyster Tytus, were fixing over an old farmhouse into their estate, soon to be called Ashintully. She made a diary entry for August 15, 1904: "Mark Twain (Sam Clemens) came with Richard Watson Gilder and spent afternoon. M.T. sat on newly painted Piazza, ruined his trousers and told funny stories for 2 hours."

Glencote and Four Brooks Farm are privately owned.

COMIC STRIPPERS

Experts in visual humor have called Berkshire home.

Harry Lambert (1916–2004) plotted action and wrote dialogue for comic books. In 1940, several years before he retired to Lenox, he worked with artist Gardner Fox to create the hero The Flash for DC comics. (The Flash had his own TV show on the CW network in autumn 2014.) Lambert also wrote the newspaper strip *Digby* in 1949.

Eliott Caplin (1913–2000) came up with the plots and words for the syndicated newspaper comic *The Heart of Juliet Jones* beginning in 1953. Stan Drake was the artist for that series. Caplin, whose brother was Al Capp, creator of *Li'l Abner*, also wrote *Peter Scratch*, *Big Ben Bolt*, *Abbie an' Slats*, *Little Orphan Annie* and other now-gone comics. A later assignment was the stories for *Encyclopedia Brown*, drawn by Frank Bolle from 1978 to 1980. Caplin retired to Stockbridge.

L. Franklin Van Zelm (1895–1961) was best known for the *Farnsworth* comic strip for the Bell Syndicate, though he wrote and drew *Rusty and Bub*, *Aw, What's the Use*, *Such Is Life*, *The Villagers* and *It's Just as True Today* (based on Bible verses). Van Zelm was a staff artist for the *Christian Science Monitor* and drew *The Vangnomes* for that paper. He and his wife, Marie, moved to Williamstown a year before his death.

Peter Laird (b. 1954), a North Adams native and 1972 graduate of Drury High School, with Kevin Eastman created the Teenage Mutant Ninja Turtles in 1984 in a self-published black-and-white comic book. The quartet of martial arts–practicing, radiation-exposed reptiles took off like a rocket—appearing in animated TV shows and films, the most recent in 2014.

JACK COLE'S ZANY PLASTIC MAN

By any stretch of the imagination, Jack Cole's Plastic Man was a burst of freshness among 1940s hyper-muscular comic book heroes who took themselves very seriously.

"The flexible red-clad crimebuster is one of the handful of heroes to have survived from the heyday of comic books, but he was never the media and merchandising hit that Superman, Batman, and Wonder Woman are," explained Ron Goulart. "That's Jack Cole's fault, since his quirky style and personality were essential to Plastic Man's complete success. The basic notion of a pliable hero who can assume any shape is a strong and appealing one, but nobody's ever been able to do it the way Jack Cole did."

Jack Ralph Cole (1914–1958) was born in New Castle, Pennsylvania. He was one of the "Coles from New Castle," he told friends. The son of a song-and-dance entertainer and a teacher, he displayed an early talent for drawing and enrolled in the Landon School of Cartooning. After a seven-thousand-mile bicycle trip across the country in 1932, he eloped with his childhood sweetheart, Dorothy Mahoney. The sale of a cartoon to *Boys' Life*

Plastic Man creator Jack Cole drew a self-portrait. Berkshire Courier, *1945.*

set him on a professional course. He soon had assignments from comic book companies. Cole in 1940 drew adventures of Silver Streak and Dickie Dare, Boy Inventor at Everett "Busy" Arnold's Quality comics group. Cole drew adventures of Quicksilver for *National Comics,* Death Patrol for *Military* and Midnight for *Smash Comics.*

Cole came up with Plastic Man in 1941. Plas, as his blubbery sidekick Woozy Winks called him, appeared in 102 issues of *Police Comics* and 64 issues of his own title. Goulart said the artist's "humor alternated between broad slapstick and quiet kidding, and there was sometimes a perverse and nasty touch to it."

The Coles rented an apartment in Great Barrington and later lived in New Marlborough. Cole said he settled in the country so there would be fewer distractions. Cole wrote and drew Plastic Man through the early 1950s. He ghosted Will Eisner's *Spirit* daily newspaper adventures. He also sold panel cartoons to *Collier's*, *Judge* and a fledgling periodical, *Playboy*. The Coles moved to Chicago in 1955 when assignments from the latter publication became steady. It was there that Cole landed the goal of his career: a contract in 1958 with the Chicago *Sun-Times* syndicate to produce a regular newspaper comic strip, *Betsy and Me*.

Then Cole's career came to an abrupt end. He inexplicably took his own life.

X
DRAMATISTS

The Berkshires is known for its summer—and, increasingly, year-round—theater and its top-notch playwrights.

William Gibson (1914–2009) came to Stockbridge in the 1950s when his psychologist wife, Margaret Brenman-Gibson, joined the staff at the Austen Riggs Center. Gibson wrote poetry and a novel (*The Cobweb* in 1954) but is best known for his stage plays *The Miracle Worker* (1959, adapted from a 1957 *Playhouse 90* script, adapted for film in 1962) and *Two for the Seesaw* (1956). During the 1960s, Gibson was president of the Berkshire Theater Festival. He wrote *The Butterfingers Angel, Mary & Joseph, Herod the Nut & the Slaughter of 12 Carols in a Pear Tree* and the Passion play *The Body & The Wheel* for the Vineyard Community in Lenox in 1974. *Monday After the Miracle*, a sequel to *Miracle Worker*, opened in 1982, a year after *Golda*, about the Israeli prime minister.

Sidney Howard (1891–1939), an ambulance driver during World War I and later an editor with *Life*, crafted the Pulitzer Prize–winning play *They Knew What They Wanted* (1925). He adapted Sinclair Lewis's *Arrowsmith* (1931) and *Dodsworth* (1936) for film. He reshaped Humphrey Cobb's *Paths of Glory* for the theater (1935). He spent considerable time at his seven-hundred-acre farm in Tyringham, where he equipped his dairy barn with Frigidaire coolers. He died when his tractor pinned him against a garage wall. His screenplay for Margaret Mitchell's *Gone with the Wind* won a posthumous Academy Award in 1939.

A novel by Thornton Wilder (1897–1975), *The Bridge of San Luis Rey* (1927), won the Pulitzer Prize. He wrote *The Seven Deadly Sins* and *The Seven Ages of*

Broadway playwright William Gibson of Stockbridge also wrote a Passion play for the Vineyard Catholic community in Lenox. *Author's collection.*

Man while staying at the Red Lion Inn in Stockbridge. He played the role of the stage manager in his *Our Town* (1938) at Berkshire Playhouse in 1939 and Williamstown Summer Theatre in 1959. He also played in his other Pulitzer Prize winner, *The Skin of Our Teeth* (1942), in Stockbridge in 1948.

Playwright, radio scriptwriter and poet Dorothy Worthington Butts (1897–1985) served with U.S. Naval Intelligence during World War I. She came to Egremont in 1948 with her husband, Bradford C. Durfee, and they restored the Old Egremont Inn. Her play *Eastward in Eden* (1947) was based on the life of Emily Dickinson; when produced on Broadway, it starred Beatrice Straight of New Marlborough. Butts published a collection of poems entitled *Berkshire Primer* (1980).

William Inge (1913–1973), known for *Come Back Little Sheba* (1949) and *Bus Stop* (1955), won the Pulitzer Prize for *Picnic* (1953). The Williamstown Theatre staged *Picnic* in 1955. He also wrote two novels. He was a member of the Williamstown Theater Festival board and of the Stockbridge Playhouse board. He had a home in Stockbridge.

XI

VERSIFIERS AND LYRICISTS

Poets and More Poets

With novels, there's an expectation of 200 or so pages of prose. With poetry, a publication could range from a several-page, hand-bound chapbook to Louise Gluck's 656-page *Poems, 1962–2012* (2013). With dozens and dozens of Berkshire poets, choices had to be made. We'll proceed alphabetically.

The English poet and critic Matthew Arnold (1822–1888) summered at Laurel Cottage in Stockbridge in 1886. He toted water from the Housatonic River, according to Richard Wilcox, and planted a tree in the yard. Henry Dwight Sedgwick said, "What a delight it was to those who chanced to be his neighbors, after looking somewhat apprehensively at the classic poet and relentless critic who had dropped from Oxford into their New England nook, to find instead the tender husband, the fond father, the kind friend, and the appreciative and grateful guest!" Arnold reminisced, "A dear girl called Emily Tuckerman took Nelly and me to a river meadow yesterday where we could find the Cardinal flower."

Mountain Farm: Poems from the Berkshire Hills (1985), by *Berkshire Eagle* "Our Berkshires" columnist Morgan G. Bulkeley III (1912–2012), appeared in 1985. His verses were frequently compared to Robert Frost's. Bulkeley was born in Hartford, graduated from Yale and raised potatoes in Mount Washington.

Lenox resident Karen Chase is represented in several anthologies. She was short-listed for Best Indie Poetry Book of 2000 for *Kazimierz Square*.

Amy Clampitt (1920–1994) of Manhattan and Lenox was "known for her dense, ornate and allusive poetry," according to an obituary. Her first full-length book was *The Kingfisher* (1983). Clampitt worked for Oxford University Press and National Audubon Society, later becoming a freelance writer and researcher. She was an editor at Dutton from 1977 to 1982. *Collected Poems* was issued in 1997. The Amy Clampitt Fund issues awards in her honor annually.

Peter Filkins of Cheshire, a graduate of Williams and Columbia, teaches at Simon's Rock. He is known both for his poetry (*The View We're Granted* the most recent, in 2012) and his translations of German works (such as H.G. Adler's *Panorama* in 2011).

The twentieth president of the United States, James A. Garfield (1831–1881), had several Berkshire connections. He attended Williams College. He submitted a verse, "To Hattie," to the *Berkshire Courier* in Great Barrington, which published it on August 31, 1854. The poem answered an earlier one by Hattie A. Pease that Garfield had read in the newspaper while visiting relatives in Monterey. Garfield's forty-five-line verse was signed "A Stranger." Pease responded two weeks later with another poem. Garfield was assassinated only four months into office. The town of Monterey changed the name of its Lake Brewer to Lake Garfield in commemoration.

David Giannini of Becket (before that, Otis and Williamstown) has been published by several small presses and literary anthologies and has received awards from the New England Foundation of the Arts and the Massachusetts Artists Foundation. He has taught poetry writing courses and workshops. He has been a rare book dealer, mental health worker and coordinator for a traveling theater group. *Span of Thread: Collected Prosepoems* came out in 2014.

Berkshire Eagle columnist Michelle Gillett of Stockbridge received an Artists Fellowship Program of the Massachusetts Council on Arts and the Humanities in 1979. She has taught English and women's studies at Miss Hall's School in Pittsfield. A recent chapbook is *The Green Cottage* (2010).

Brothers Michael (1949–2010) and Peter (b. 1959) Gizzi grew up in Pittsfield, where their father worked for GE Transformer. Michael twice won the Gertrude Stein Award for Innovative Writing. Several books of his poetry have been published, including *carmela bianca* (1974). Peter won the 1994 Lavan Younger Poet Award from the Academy of American Poets.

Once a lecturer in English at Williams College, now at Yale, New York City–born Louise Gluck (b. 1943) won a Guggenheim Memorial Fellowship in 1987. She was U.S. poet laureate in 2003–04. Her collections of verse include the award-winning *The Triumph of Achilles* (1985). Gluck won the

Pulitzer Prize for poetry in 1993 for *The Wild Iris. Faithful and Virtuous Night: Poems* came out in 2014.

Gerald Hausman (b. 1945), the author of *Sitting on the Blue-Eyed Bear: Navajo Myths and Legends* and other works of poetry, lived in Monterey from 1968 to 1977. He taught at Mountain School in Stockbridge and was poet-in-residence in the Pittsfield schools. Other books include *New Marlboro Stage* (1969), *Circle Meadow* (1972) and *The Boy with the Sun Tree Bow* (1973).

Stockbridge resident Robert Underwood Johnson (1853–1937) was an editor with *Century Magazine* and ambassador to Italy under President Woodrow Wilson. His *Poems* (1908) includes "To the Housatonic at Stockbridge."

Margery Mansfield (1895–1984) of Monterey edited *American Women Poets* (1937) and published *Berkshire Settler* (1961).

Edna St. Vincent Millay (1892–1950) was the first female poet to win the Pulitzer Prize, for *The Harp-Weaver and Other Poems* (1923). Partially named for New York's St. Vincent Hospital, she was born in Maine and graduated from Vassar in 1917, the same year her first collection, *Renascence and Other Poems*, came out. Known for her liberated views and hedonistic lifestyle, she and her husband, Eugene Jan Boissevain, made 650-acre Steepletop in Austerlitz, New York, their home for twenty-five years. Her small writing cabin is on the grounds. The *New York Times* said: "Edna St. Vincent Millay was a terse and moving spokesman during the Twenties, the Thirties and the Forties. She was an idol of the younger generation during the glorious early days of Greenwich Village when she wrote, what critics termed a frivolous but widely know poem which ended: My candle burns at both ends, It will not last the night; But ah, my foes, and oh, my friends, It gives a lovely light!"

Edna St. Vincent Millay's Steepletop is a house museum today. *Library of Congress.*

The poet's sister, actress and singer Norma Millay Ellis (1894–1986), in 1973 established the Millay Colony for the Arts on part of the property. Today the Edna St. Vincent Millay Society maintains Steepletop and its garden and offers tours.

William Pitt Palmer (1805–1884) was born in Stockbridge and later lived in Pittsfield. He attended Williams College and Berkshire Medical Institute in Pittsfield. Though he also studied law, he became a teacher and writer. He was later president of an insurance company. He read one of his earliest poems before the Anti-Slavery Society at Williams in 1828. "To the New Moon, Passing Behind Monument Mountain, Stockbridge, Mass." appeared in *Graham's Magazine* in 1846. His book *Echoes of Half a Century* (1880) was dedicated to Mark Hopkins and included "Lines on Revisiting Berkshire Late in Autumn." Palmer's comic poem "The Smack in School" is modeled on the Little Red Schoolhouse in the Larrywaug section of Stockbridge. "Smack" was first carried in the *Pittsfield Sun* for November 18, 1858, just after Palmer had read it for the Literary Society in Stockbridge.

Works by Congregational minister, poet and shepherd Stephen Philbrick of Windsor—the son of "New England Suite" poet Charles Horace Philbrick—include *Up to the Elbow* (1997) and *Backyard Lumberjack* (2006).

Pittsfield native Lawrence Raab (b. 1946) taught at Williams College. His poetry has included *The Poetry Miscellany* (1972), *Mysteries of the Horizon* (1972), *The Collector of Cold Weather* (1976), *Other Children* (1987) and *Under One Roof* (1992). *What We Don't Know About Each Other* came out in 1995. He earned a Guggenheim Fellowship in 2007. His recent work is *The History of Forgetting* (2009).

Williams faculty member David L. Smith (b. 1954) published a collection of new and selected poems, *Civil Rights* (1996), under the pen name "D.L. Crockett-Smith." It included poems from the 1970s, '80s and '90s exploring autobiographical, historical, cultural and political themes. The black poet's work has appeared in several anthologies.

A former poet-in-residence at Williams College (1959–63) and frequent lecturer there, William Jay Smith (b. 1918) is an editor and translator and is fluent in seven languages. His first book of verse was *Poems* (1947). He was one of three poets to speak at a William Cullen Bryant bicentennial celebration at the Homestead in 1994. He was U.S. poet laureate in 1968–70. He lives in Cummington and Paris, France.

A poem by Mormon Eliza Roxcy Snow (1804–1887), "Great Is the Lord," became a hymn. The Becket native in 1842 married Latter Day Saints founder Joseph Smith Jr. After Smith was stoned to death two years later, she married his successor, Brigham Young. In both cases she was a plural wife.

Barry Sternlieb of Richmond, whose works include *Thoreau's Hat* (1994) and *Winter Crows* (2009), is publisher of Mad River Press. He won the 2004 Massachusetts Cultural Council Fellowship in Poetry.

Great Barrington brothers Charles Allen Sumner (1835–1903) and Samuel Barstow Sumner (1832–1891) were both featured in *Poems* (1877). Charles graduated from Trinity College and was a shorthand reporter and lawyer. He commanded the First Nevada Infantry volunteers with the rank of colonel and eventually became a member and president pro tem of the Nevada Senate. He edited several daily newspapers, including the *San Francisco Mirror*. Samuel graduated from Williams College and was admitted to the Berkshire bar in 1852. He served with the Forty-ninth Massachusetts Regiment in the Civil War and was wounded at Port Huron in 1863. He was city attorney, judge and clerk of courts in Bridgeport, Connecticut. His poems were printed in the *Berkshire Courier* during his days here.

Great Barrington–born Charles Allen Sumner was a lawyer and a poet. He and his brother Samuel Barstow Sumner co-authored a collection of poetry. Poems, *1877*.

Teacher, critic, translator, Pulitzer Prize–winning poet (in 1956 for *Things of This World* and in 1989 for *New and Collected Poems*) and U.S. poet laureate (1987–88) Richard Wilbur (b. 1921) lives in Cummington. "I always felt that there was a particular enchantment about the Berkshire area and the foothills of the Berkshires where we are now," he told the *Sunday Republican*. Wilbur was

Richard Wilbur, an American poet laureate, spoke at a bicentennial event just up the road from his Cummington home, at the William Cullen Bryant Homestead. *Bernard A. Drew, 1994.*

born in New York City and grew up on a farm in New Jersey. He studied at Amherst College and Harvard University. He served with the Thirty-sixth Infantry Division in Italy during World War II. Wilbur was principal lyricist for Leonard Bernstein's musical *Candide*. He spoke at the William Cullen Bryant Bicentennial Celebration event at the Bryant Homestead in 1994.

ANNIE KILMER'S TREE-HUGGING SON JOYCE

Joyce Kilmer (1886–1918) wrote the verse "Trees" (1913), which still rolls easily from many a tongue. The poet more than once visited his mother when she summered in Cheshire.

Joyce was one of four children of Annie (1861–1931) and her husband, Dr. F.B. Kilmer. After her children had grown, Annie Kilmer gravitated to the Berkshires, close to her native Albany, New York. The poet wrote to his mother in 1916: "It must be nice to see Mt. Graylock [*sic*], a most excellent mountain, as I remember it. You should take a motor trip up through the Notch to the Bellows Pipe, if possible, and also look up Dave

Eddy, the original 'Dave Lilly.'" Kilmer is talking about his poem "Dave Lilly," which is about a North Adams idler who would rather fish than toil in the field.

Kilmer paid a flying visit soon after this, as his mother wrote in her diary: "On the 29th of May I left home for Cheshire, Mass., where I had arranged to spend the summer months. I had luncheon with Joyce at Henri's and we went to the matinee at the Palace Theatre [in Pittsfield]."

Following Joyce's death in action during World War I, Annie stayed periodically in South Egremont and Great Barrington and wrote her own poetry ("The War Mother") and dedicated trees (including one on the North Egremont village green in 1930) and otherwise kept the flame of her son's memory burning.

SONGWRITERS

What lyric by a young Berkshire girl has been set to music no fewer than thirteen times? The first of the songs was composed in 1892, the latest in 2003. A version was performed at the Chicago World's Fair in 1893 and was recorded by the tenor Henry Burr in 1907. It's Elaine Goodale's "Ashes of Roses," a verse from *Apple-Blossoms*. Goodale wrote in her autobiography that the poem "has since been repeatedly set to music and sung in concerts by famous artists. I have rather resented the fact that these melodious but quite trivial lines have been chosen to represent me in various anthologies." The most recent version is a forty-minute opus in six movements for choir and orchestra by Jocelyn Hagen.

None paid Elaine a cent in royalty.

Nor did Bryant profit when Winthrop Rogers set "To a Waterfowl" to music in 1919, four decades after the poet's death.

Longfellow recommended "The Old Clock on the Stairs" when asked which of his works was best suited to musical adaptation in 1846. Several versions followed.

A century ago, pianists and singers acquired popular sheet music such as Ben Chadwick's *The Grand Old Berkshire Hills* (1903) or *(I Lost My Heart to a Wonderful Girl) In the Heart of the Berkshire Hills* (1918) by Clyde Hager and Walter Goodwin or Wells Hastings and Mary Schaeffer's *The Song of the Berkshire Hills* (1955).

Here's a sampling of other Berkshire lyrics writers:

George F. Root (1820–1895) wrote "Just Before the Battle, Mother" and "Tramp, Tramp, Tramp, the Boys Are Marching"—widely popular tunes during the Civil War, at least in the North. Southerners put their own words to the tune of "The Battle Cry of Freedom." Born in Sheffield, Root studied organ and choral music and was a teacher as well as performer. In 1859, he joined his younger brother E.T. Root, who ran a music store in Chicago. The composer of some two hundred songs, Root returned to Sheffield for a church anniversary in 1876.

Washington Gladden composed "The Mountains" at the time he was a member of the Williams College class of 1859. It is said to be the oldest college song in the country. He noted in his memoirs, "One winter morning, walking down Bee Hill, the lilt of the chorus of 'The Mountains' came to me. I had a little music-paper in my room in the village, and on my arrival I wrote down the notes. Then I cast about for words to fit them, and the refrain 'The Mountains, the Mountains!' suggested itself."

While at Yale, Cole Porter (1891–1964) wrote the football songs "Bingo Eli Yale" and "Bulldog." The songsmith became known for his urbane, witty lyrics in such musicals as *Gay Divorcee* (1932), *Anything Goes* (1934) and *Can-Can* (1953). The last of Porter's eight hundred songs were for *Silk Stockings* in 1955. Porter and his wife, Linda, became part-time residents of Buxton Hill, Williamstown, in 1940 so he could recuperate from a riding accident. He wrote *Kiss Me, Kate* (1948) here. Porter bequeathed the property to Williams College, which sold it in 1966.

Great Barrington songwriter Aaron Schroeder (1926–2009) composed "Way Back When Is Back Again" for the Great Barrington Town Hall bandstand in 1987. Far better known, of course, is "It's Now or Never," which he co-wrote with Wally Gold. Recorded by Elvis Presley, it aced the charts for five weeks in 1960. Schroeder wrote seventeen Top 20 hits for Presley.

Arlo Guthrie (b. 1947), son of folk music legend Woody Guthrie, lives in the town of Washington. The Guthrie Foundation owns the former Trinity Church in VanDeusenville, Great Barrington, scene of the famous Thanksgiving Day trash disposal debacle that prompted the eighteen-minute ballad "Alice's Restaurant Massacree" (1965) and a subsequent motion picture. Guthrie in winter 2015 set off on an eighteen-month, fiftieth anniversary tour showcasing the Vietnam War–era classic. Guthrie's "Massachusetts" became the commonwealth's official folk song in 1981. His children's book, *Mooses Come Walking* (1995), illustrated by Alice Brock, sold out its first printing. Still fascinated by moose, he wrote *Whose Moose Am I?* in 2014.

You can get anything you want at Alice's Restaurant, folk singer Arlo Guthrie wrote in 1965. He played at the Boys' Club in Pittsfield at the start of his career. *Glen Boyd photo/ courtesy Donna Drew.*

James Taylor (b. 1948) lives in New Lenox, on the other side of October Mountain from Guthrie. A near-annual attraction at Tanglewood in recent years, the singer's "Sweet Baby James" (1970) always brings the crowd to its feet. The song of course mentions the Berkshires; Taylor wrote it during a stay at the Austen Riggs Center in Stockbridge in 1970.

JAMES WELDON JOHNSON AND THE NEGRO NATIONAL ANTHEM

James Weldon Johnson (1871–1938) in the 1920s purchased a summer place in the Seekonk section of Great Barrington called Five Acres. He was a frequent visitor to the Mason Library, where he prepared parts of *God's Trombones: Seven Negro Sermons in Verse* (1927). This was before he completed the cozy writing cabin on his property.

Johnson was introduced to the area by Mary White Ovington (1865–1951), one of the founders of the National Association for the Advancement of Colored People who summered in Alford for two decades at a property she called Riverbank. White wrote juvenile books such as *Hazel* (1912) and *Zeke* (1930)—the last penned here.

Johnson was the first black attorney admitted to the Florida bar since the Civil War. He, brother J. Rosamund Johnson and Bob Cole collaborated in writing popular songs and light opera. The Johnson brothers' "Lift Every Voice and Sing" (1900) was adopted as the NAACP national anthem. Johnson served for many years as field secretary for the NAACP. He taught at Fisk University and New York University.

Johnson told the *Berkshire Courier*:

> *Writing is one of the world's hardest jobs. You become a slave to your sense of duty. When you want to knock off for the afternoon, it is necessary that you whip yourself to stay at your desk. You can't get away from your job, as a hardware merchant can…Another rule for one's ultimate success in literature is the drudgery of rewriting. Everything that goes out from here (he indicated his little studio workshop, hidden in the pines on the bank of the Seekonk brook) is written three times. By the time the last draft is out of the typewriter, the chances are that I've said about what I intended to.*

Both Five Acres and Riverbank are privately owned today.

THE MERRY BOLTWOOD-LIDDLE OPERETTAS

Two Pittsfield men, Frederick J. Liddle and Edward Boltwood, wrote the music and words, respectively, for *Sunny Sicily*, a light opera that was staged at both the Colonial Theatre in Pittsfield and the Mahaiwe Theater in Great

Barrington in 1905. One of the performers was Joseph McArthur Vance, architect for both theaters.

The plot? Heroine Agatha Sweetfern is betrothed to Benjamin Raspberry, chief selectman. Great Britain and the United States are at war—it's 1812. A single British prisoner, Captain Reginald McIntosh, is in custody in Pittsfield. (There really was a prisoner of war camp on upper North Street.) Raspberry can't concentrate on preparing for marriage, as Colonel Beacon Hill is about to make an official inspection of the prison. But McIntosh has escaped. So there will be no bad report, Raspberry disguises himself as McIntosh. Then the real McIntosh returns in the guise of a gypsy. And McIntosh-the-gypsy falls in love with Agatha. If you've seen a Gilbert & Sullivan operetta, you get the idea.

Boltwood (1870–1934) invited Englishman Liddle (1858–1914), director of the Pittsfield Symphony Orchestra, to compose new music to a play for which Boltwood had written lyrics while at Yale, *Henry Number 8*. The collaboration continued with *Happy Day*, *Sunny Sicily*, *Princess Runaway*, *The Silver Sword* and *The Red Lady*.

Boltwood had worked for *Harper's* magazine and for the Pittsburgh *Dispatch*. Returning to his native Pittsfield, he wrote a history of the city for the years 1876–1916 and contributed short stories and verse to *Century* and other periodicals.

Liddle died of a heart attack. Boltwood's passing was more dramatic. On an evening excursion, he tumbled six feet from a bridge in New Lebanon, New York, struck his head and apparently died instantly; his body was not found until the next morning.

XII

BIBLIOPHILIC TREASURES—AND THE ODDEST BERKSHIRE NOVEL

Bibliophiles seek many works by the authors we've shelved in our dream libraries. Generally a first edition, first impression, publisher's cloth with pristine original dust jacket would command the highest price. A signed copy? Better yet.

Books that have been particularly elusive of my bibliophilic searches are *not* by the best-known writers, and that's perhaps why they've been so elusive.

• Clay Perry and John L.E. Pell's *Hell's Acres*, a tale of horse thievery described earlier, was published in hardcover in February 1938 by Lee Furman Inc.—the publisher calling it "probably the most outstanding novel I have ever issued." A relative of one of the darker characters portrayed in the book is rumored to have purchased and destroyed most of the copies and the printing plates. The book is 8vo (if you are puzzled by this term, it is bibliophilic jargon for octavo, or a book with pages five by eight inches), four hundred pages, red cloth cover. The dust jacket shows a scene outside the Black Grocery Tavern. An 1853 map illustrates the endpapers. I have a photocopy.

• Elaine Goodale Eastman's last and most ambitious novel, *Hundred Maples* (1935), published by Stephen Daye Press of Brattleboro, Vermont, is about three women who make very different life choices. It took me decades to find a copy with dust jacket (showing four trees and their shadows). It is 8vo, 286 pages, green cloth.

• Three of Anthony M. Rud's supernatural Jigger Masters novels appeared in Macaulay hardcover editions. *The Rose Bath Riddle* (1934), originally serialized in *Detective Fiction Weekly* beginning on October 7, 1933, is 254 pages, blue cloth. The dust jacket has blood-red lettering over the scene of a man desperate to get out of a shower. *House of the Damned* (1934) was called "The Death Messenger" when it appeared in *Two Book Detective Magazine*, February–March 1934. The dust jacket depicts green silhouetted figures, 256 pages, orange-ish cloth cover. The author's name is correct on the dust jacket but misspelled on the title page as "Rudd." *The Stuffed Men* (1935), in *DFW* beginning on January 20, 1934, is 250 pages, yellow or blue cloth cover (I've seen both). The dust jacket shows the faces of three characters superimposed over skulls. A signed copy was recently offered for $595. I've long had copies of the first and third books. Finally, after thirty years looking, I acquired an affordable middle volume. All are 8vo. All of my copies are beat up. I acquired new wrappers for all three from Facsimile Dust Jackets LLC.

Another book I've sought is even more of a curiosity than Harlan Ballard's Masonic novel.

• Charles Sheldon French (1856–1914), who was born in Peru, lived in Hinsdale, moved from the area and then spent the last fourteen years of his life in Dalton. He "was a person fond of literature and had done considerable writing," according to the *Pittsfield Journal*. His *The Worship of the Golden Calf* (1908) argues pro-labor politics. Subtitled "A Story of Wage Slavery in Massachusetts," its setting is a barely disguised Dalton (called Papyrus) and its two paper mills owned by the despicable Baldwins (Cranes) and the more likable Wessons (Westons).

The plot is about honest Jon Wycliff and his struggle against repressive labor practices by the Baldwins. The author decries long hours, poor working conditions, low pay, vindictiveness, manipulation of town government, control of the press, corruption of the church and false generosity. And that's only the start.

"How have the Baldwins made their millions?" the writer asks.

> *Of course the whole world knows that they make a very high grade of paper. It is said that this is due, in some measure, to the pure water found in Papyrus, which is the gift of God. Then, too, it is claimed that Mack Baldwin laid the foundation of the Baldwin millions by manipulations in Wall Street, during the Civil War. But some of those millions are the fruit of low wages. If the Baldwins pay twenty five cents a day less than a fair wage, what is the result? It's a yearly savings of one hundred and fifty thousand dollars, of money due the laborers, is it not?*

French considered himself a political progressive, which in the era of muckraking journalism and revelations of bribery and business scandal stood for safety and sanitation codes and other civic programs. French stopped short of advocating labor unions—he slightly predates that movement.

It has been suggested, but not substantiated, that members of the Crane family acquired and destroyed most copies of the book.

Worship of the Golden Calf is 8vo, 190 pages, blue cloth, no dust jacket. A digitized version may be downloaded free from the Internet.

SELECTED BIBLIOGRAPHY

Anderson, Gidske. *Sigrid Undset, et liv*. Oslo, Norway: Gyldendal Norsk Forlag, 1989.

Appleton's Encyclopedia of American Biography. David Hitchcock entry. New York: D. Appleton, 1900.

Ashley, Mike. *The Mammoth Encyclopedia of Modern Crime Fiction*. New York: Carroll & Graf, 2002.

Aurora Beacon-News. "C.P. Burton's Latest Book Called Best." September 23, 1928.

Bales, Jack. "Charles Pierce Burton & the Boys of Bob's Hill." *Boy's Book Buff* no. 5, February 1978.

Bass, Milton. "Writing No Mystery to These Authors." *Berkshire Eagle*, December 20, 2008.

Beacon-News. Charles Pierce Burton interview. October 21, 1934.

Beck, Lesley Ann. "Local Novelist Robb Forman Dew." *Berkshires Monthly*, January 24, 2002.

Berkshire Courier. "Afternoon with a Literateur [James Weldon Johnson]." September 9, 1937.

———. Harriet Beecher Stowe in Great Barrington news item. October 9, 16 and 23, 1872.

———. "Mark Twain." November 1, 1871.

———. "William C. Bryant's Habits." May 31, 1871.

Berkshire Eagle. "Amy Clampitt, Poet, Dead at 74." September 12, 1994.

———. "Arrowhead Getting New Piazza." July 29, 1977.

————. "Late Author [MacKinley Kantor] Is Recalled as Frequent Area Visitor." October 12, 1977.

————. "Mark Twain's Daughter Has Narrow Escape from Death." August 1, 1904.

————. "Sally Lagerlof Is Model of Stockbridge Kitchen Maid Who Won $1100 for Writing Novel." October 19, 1936.

Berkshire Evening Eagle. "Mrs. Wharton's Chauffeur First Person to Climb Greylock in Car." September 10, 1937.

————. "Perry, Back Home, Tells of Night in Wild Hills." February 22, 1938.

————. "Piazza of Melville Home Sold to Judge Pitney of New Jersey." November 18, 1937.

————. "Replica of Hawthorne's House Will Be Dedicated Next Year." August 7, 1947.

————. "William Cullen Bryant Set in Verse Murder Which Took Place on an Old Berkshire Way." April 6, 1929.

Berkshire Gleaner. Mark Twain. Undated clipping, scrapbook, Lee Library.

Berkshire Hills. "Oliver Wendell Holmes." October 1, 1902.

Billings, Josh. *Josh Billings, His Sayings.* New York: Carleton, 1871.

Birdsall, Richard D. *Berkshire County: A Cultural History.* New Haven, CT: Yale University Press, 1959.

Brooks, Van Wyck. *The Flowering of New England.* New York: E.P. Dutton, 1936.

Brunjes, Ann. "The American Struggle for Identity in 18th Century Newspaper Verse." *Bridgewater Review* 17, no. 1 (June 1998).

Bulkeley, Morgan. "Henry James in the Berkshires." *Berkshire Eagle*, October 12, 1961.

Burton, Charles Pierce. "Author Reveals Romance Source," letter. *Evening Transcript*, November 22, 1932.

Carman, Bernard. "Berkshire Bookshelf: Hawthorne Notes North Adams." *Berkshire Eagle*, July 9, 1960.

Chapman, Gerard. *William Cullen Bryant: The Cummington Years.* Milton, MA: The Trustees of Reservations, 1980.

Connerton, Dan. "Nathaniel Hawthorne: The North Adams Years." *Berkshire Sampler*, September 14, 1980.

Cooke, Rose Terry. "The Adventures of Rose Terry Cooke's Best Story." *Springfield Daily Republican*, December 26, 1878.

Cutler, James Tucker. "The Literary Associations of Berkshire." *New England Magazine*, September 1893.

Drew, Bernard A. "Berkshires in Song: Old Sheet Music." *Dalton News-Record*, October 7, 1981.

———. "Thoreau's Tarn Identified: Gilder Pond." *Concord Saunterer* 9 (2001).

Eastman, Elaine Goodale. *Sister to the Sioux*. Lincoln: University of Nebraska Press, 1978.

Eaton, Walter Prichard. "The Hawthorne House." *Stockbridge*, August 1, 1914.

Esteemed Correspondent (Cornelius Mathews). "Several Days in Berkshire." *Literary World*, August 24 and 31 and September 7, 1850.

Fall, Kingsley R. "Many Berkshire Writers Are Represented in Field of Juvenile Literature." *Berkshire Eagle*, November 10, 1934.

F., D.D. (Field, David Dudley, Jr.). "Journey of a Day." *United States Magazine and Democratic Review*, October 1844.

Fields, James T. *Yesterdays with Authors*. New York: Osgood & Co., 1873.

Gilder, Cornelia Brooke, with Julia Conklin Peters. *Hawthorne's Lenox: The Tanglewood Circle*. Charleston, SC: The History Press, 2008.

Goulart, Ron. *Focus on Jack Cole*. Seattle, WA: Fantagraphic Books, 1986.

Gulick, Bill. *Sixty-Four Years as a Writer by Bill Gulick, Who Survived Them*. Caldwell, ID: Caxton Press, 2006.

Happel, Richard V. Hugh C. Wheeler profile. *Berkshires Week*, August 2, 1979.

———. Notes and Footnotes. *Berkshire Eagle*, October 3, 1949.

Harper, Katherine Ann. "The Man from Muscatine: A Bio-bibliography of Ellis Parker Butler." PhD dissertation. Ann Arbor, MI: Bowling Green State University, 2000.

Hawthorne, Nathaniel. *Twenty Days with Julian and Bunny*. New York: Review Books, 2003.

Hayward, C.S. "Tyringham Tradition Abounds in Stories of Mark Twain." *Springfield Republican*, February 4, 1945.

Highsmith, Patricia. *Plotting and Writing Suspense Fiction*. New York: St. Martin's, 2001.

Huber, Parker J. *Elevating Ourselves: Thoreau on Mountains*. New York: Mariner Books, 1999.

Jarenski, Shelly. "A Revival of Rachel Field's Hitty." *Advocate,* January 5, 2000.

Katz, Judy. "The Fireplace Melville Wrote by Is Found." *Berkshire Eagle*, May 29, 1977.

Kennedy, Louise. "Playwright [Joan Ackermann], Entire Company Get in on the Act." *Boston Globe,* June 10, 2005.

Knickerbocker. Boy of Mount Rhigi review. November 1848.

Kunitz, Stanley J., and Howard Haycraft. *Twentieth Century Authors*. New York: H.W. Wilson, 1943.

Kuperschmid, Eileen. "Stepping into Success: Williamstown's Thayer: 'Everything Is Christmas.'" *Berkshire Sampler,* January 10, 1982.

La Fontana, John. "Meet the Creator of 'Plastic Man.'" *Berkshire Courier*, December 6, 1945.

Lawrence, Arthur. "Bryant and the Berkshire Hills." *Century Magazine*, June 1895.

Lawton, Mary. *A Lifetime with Mark Twain*. New York: Harcourt, Brace, 1925.

Lefkowitz, David. "Encounter with Joan Ackermann." *Playbill Online*, August 15, 2000.

Levine, Miriam. *A Guide to Writers' Homes in New England*. Carlisle, MA: Applewood Books, 1989.

The Log. Ben Benson profile. October 2012.

Longfellow, Samuel, ed. *Life of Henry Wadsworth Longfellow with Extracts from His Journals and Correspondence*. Boston: Houghton Mifflin, 1886.

Lukeman, Helen Bidwell. Letter to Grace Bidwell Wilcox, September 28, 1953, courtesy Richard Wilcox.

Mainiero, Lina, ed. *American Women Writers: A Critical Reference Guide from Colonial Times to the Present*. New York: Ungar, 1981.

Mallary, R. DeWitt. "Lenox in Literature." *Critic*, July 1902.

Mansfield, Luther Stearns, ed. "Glimpses of Herman Melville's Life in Pittsfield 1850–51: Some Unpublished Letters of Evert A. Duyckinck." *American Literature* 9, no. 1 (March 1937).

Miles, Lion G. "Anna Bingham: From the Red Lion Inn to the Supreme Court." *New England Quarterly* 69, no. 2 (June 1996).

————. "Jane Fitzpatrick's Gifted Predecessor," letter. *Berkshire Eagle*, November 19, 2013.

Moore, Steve. "Jory Turns 20." *Berkshire Eagle*, June 10, 1988.

Nash, Albert. "Berkshire Scenery: Mount Washington." *Housatonic Mirror*, October 28, 1846.

New York Times. "Edna St. Vincent Millay Found Dead at 58." October 20, 1950.

————. "Hawthorne's House Burned." June 29, 1890.

Niles, Grace Greylock. *The Hoosac Valley: Its Legends and Its History*. New York: G.P. Putnam's Sons, 1912.

North Adams Transcript. "Burns Night Celebration." January 31, 1895.

————. "Memorial Marker for Stockbridge." January 5, 1929.

Nunley, Richard. "Something of the Hawk-Eye [Nathaniel Hawthorne]." *Berkshire Eagle*, July 13, 1983.

————, ed. *The Berkshire Reader: Writings from New England's Secluded Paradise*. Stockbridge, MA: Berkshire House, 1992.

Peattie, Roderick, ed. *The Berkshires: The Purple Hills*. New York: Vanguard Press, 1948.

Perry, Clay. "Birthplace of 'Josh Billings' Purchased by Martin Reilly." *Springfield Republican*, November 7, 1948.

———. "Colorful Charles H. Daniels Reigned Here as Cider King." *Berkshire Eagle*, July 9, 1960.

Pincus, Andrew L. "Musician of Mystery: Tanglewood Violinist Puts His Pen to a Murder Tale." *Berkshire Eagle*, July 26, 2009.

Pittsfield Journal. Charles Sheldon French obituary. December 19, 1914.

Pittsfield Sun. "Pittsfield and Poetry." April 14, 1887.

Poutasse, Marianna. *Power of Place: Herman Melville in the Berkshires*. Charleston, SC: The History Press, 2014.

Rice, Alice Hegan. *The Inky Way*. New York: D. Appleton-Century, 1940.

Ruber, Peter. "Anthony M. Rud." *Pulp Rack*, December 2002.

Sedgwick, Henry Dwight. "Reminiscences of Literary Berkshire." *Century Magazine*, August 1895.

Sedgwick, Sarah Cabot, and Christina Sedgwick Marquand. *Stockbridge 1739–1939: A Chronicle*. Stockbridge, MA: Sedgwick & Marquand, 1939.

Simpson, Claude M., ed. *The Local Colorists: American Short Stories, 1857–1900*. New York: Harper & Brothers, 1960.

Smith, Chard Powers. *The Housatonic: Puritan River*. New York: Rinehart & Co., 1946.

Smith, J.E.A. *The Poet Among the Hills*. Pittsfield, MA: George Blatchford, 1895.

Springfield Sunday Republican. "Pulitzer Prize–Winning Author Proves Uncommon Poet." August 3, 1986.

Sukiennik, Greg. "Becket Attic Yields Melville Trove." *Berkshire Eagle*, December 5, 1998.

Sunday Morning Call. "Another Relic." January 4, 1891.

Szasz, Ferenc Morton. *Abraham Lincoln and Robert Burns: Connected Lives and Legends*. Carbondale: Southern Illinois University Press, 2008.

Thomson, Edith Parker. "The Home of Josh Billings." *New England Magazine*, February 1898.

Wellesley magazine. Carolyn Heilbrun profile. Spring 1984.

Wharton, Edith. *A Backward Glance*. New York: Appleton-Century, 1934.

Widmer, Edward L. *Young America: The Flowering of Democracy in New York City*. New York: Oxford University Press, 1998.

Wilbur, Richard. "A Word from Cummington." In *Under Open Sky: Poets on William Cullen Bryant*, edited by Norbert Krapf. Roslyn, NY: Stone House Press, 1987.

Wilcox, Richard B. "Laurel Cottage." April 1, 2014, paper read at Stockbridge.

INDEX

ABOUT THE AUTHOR

Bernard A. Drew wallpapered two servants' rooms at the Bryant Homestead as a summer laborer; studied "The Novel of Violence" in English class with Robert B. Parker at Northeastern University; persuaded Arlo Guthrie to write a poem, "Old Bill: He's Just Ahead in Pittsfield," for a local history publication; with his wife, Donna, attended Sophia Peabody Hawthorne's reburial at Sleepy Hollow Cemetery in

Bernard A. Drew. *Darcie M. Drew.*

Concord; and ate haggis in Scotland in respect to Robbie Burns. A resident of Great Barrington, Massachusetts, he is an associate editor of the *Lakeville (CT) Journal* and is a columnist for the *Berkshire Eagle* (Pittsfield, MA). He has published thirty Berkshire histories and twenty popular literature reference books. He is a past president of the Berkshire County and Great Barrington Historical Societies and was a founding director of the Upper Housatonic Valley National Heritage Area. And he reads a lot.